JACQUES CARTIER

# JACQUES CARTIER

AND HIS

# FOUR VOYAGES TO CANADA

## AN ESSAY

WITH HISTORICAL, EXPLANATORY AND
PHILOLOGICAL NOTES

BY

HIRAM B. STEPHENS, B.C.L.

MONTREAL:
W. DRYSDALE & CO., PUBLISHERS
232 ST. JAMES STREET

GAZETTE PRINTING COMPANY, MONTREAL.

# CONTENTS.

# CONTENTS.

*Richard Hakluyt;*

*Henry*

# PREFACE.

It is a happy omen for the future of any country
when its people take a pride in its history, and
delight in studying even its earliest annals. Of late
years this patriotic spirit has been notably developed
in Canada, and the result has affected its literature in
a marked degree. No possible reason can be assigned
why an educated Canadian should neglect to acquire
a full knowledge of the history of Canada. In the
emphatic words of the late Hon. T. D. McGee:—"No
Province of any ancient or modern power—not even
Gaul when it was a Province of Rome—has had
nobler imperial names interwoven with its local
events. Under the French kings Canada was the
theatre of action for a whole series of men of first-
rate reputation—men eminent for their energy, their
fortitude, their courage and their accomplishments—
for all that constitutes and adorns civil and military
reputations. Under our English sovereigns—from
the days of Wolfe to those of the lamented Earl of
Elgin, our great names are connected with some of
the best and highest passages in the annals of the
empire. We have not, therefore, a history simply
provincial, interesting only to the provincials themselves; but a history which forms an inseparable and
conspicuous part in the annals of the best ages of the

two first empires in the world—France and England." The series of works on "France and England in North America," by Dr. Francis Parkman, has done much to stimulate our love for romantic and picturesque historical details, as well as for accurate local description; and the American historian has closely kept in view the lines that he proposed to follow, when, after gaining an intimate acquaintance with his subject from all available sources—books and manuscripts—he began his successful task. He has studied events in all their bearings on one another—near or remote—in the character, habits and manners of those who took part in them, and, in short, has, as it were, made himself a spectator of the varied incidents and actions of which he has given us so fascinating an account. Dr. Parkman's chapter on "Early French Adventure in North America," which contains his narrative of Cartier's voyages and discoveries, consists of only thirty-five pages; and, though interesting, like that all he writes, it is too brief to be quite satisfactory to the lovers of detailed biography. There is, also, a good account of Jacques Cartier, by the Rev. Dr. Benjamin F. de Costa, in Vol. IV. of the "Narrative and Critical History of America," edited by Justin Winsor. It is unnecessary here to make mention of the best histories—French and English—which, as a rule, devote considerable space to the Commodore of St. Malo. Many students, however, have long been desirous of possessing in a trustworthy English translation the complete story of the adventures of Jacques Cartier. This want will soon be adequately supplied by the publication of four essays—two in English and two in French—dedicated to the subject of the "Breton sailor, sometimes styled 'the Corsair.'" Some time ago, four medals were offered by his Honor Lieutenant-Governor Angers to competitors for prize essays on "Jacques Cartier and his Time." The medals were awarded by competent judges to Joseph Pope, Civil Service, Ottawa; to Dr. N. E. Dionne, Quebec; to Hiram B. Stephens, Montreal; and to Toüon de Longrais, Rennes, France.

It is with the third mentioned of these compositions that I have now to deal, and I will briefly draw attention to the salient points of the essay in question. Mr. Stephens himself, in a few prefatory words, informs us that " its *motif*, if it may be so called, has been to give all the facts concerning Jacques Cartier known up to the present time;" and he believes that his " pages contain everything of value now known about Cartier." First, then, an account is given of the brave explorer's life, of which, as we are all aware, not much can now be ascertained, apart from what we learn from the " Voyages." Next, Mr. Stephens has translated from the original French, " with much care and trouble," the accounts of the Canadian voyages of Jacques Cartier; and he informs us accurately of the dates when and the places where these accounts were published. At the end of each of the first two voyages he gives a vocabulary of common words " in the language of the land newly discovered." From the vocabulary attached to the second voyage, entitled " Language of the Districts and Kingdoms of Hochelaga and Canada, otherwise named by us New France," we learn that the word "Canada"occurs for the first time in that narrative, and signifies a " town or village "—" *Ils appellent une ville Canada.*" As there have been various theories regarding the origin of the name "Canada," it may be mentioned that (in addition to a short article on the word in the notes appended by Mr. Stephens to the journal of Cartier's second voyage) at p. 67 of Dr. de Costa's account of "Jacques Cartier and his Successors," numerous references are given to the works of the best writers who have discussed the meaning of the term. Dr. Parkman, also, has a note on "Canada" at page 184 of his "Pioneers of France in the New World."

Mr. Stephens has added to his translations a large number of notes on the voyages, and these, having been, as a rule, carefully condensed, must have cost the writer considerable time and trouble. In his notes to the third voyage, while referring to the story of Roberval's niece, who was put ashore on the "Isle of Demons," with her lover and old nurse, Mr. Stephens remarks:—"Modern writers have used the incident—among them, I think, Frechette." He might have added that "Marguerite," by George Martin, of Montreal, is an admirable poetic version of the same ghastly legend. The essay closes with a list of recent works, which, in addition to those of older writers, are of interest to students in connection with Cartier and his voyages.

It was fitting that some Montrealer should be a competitor for the prizes offered by the Lieutenant-Governor, and we should all congratulate our fellow-townsman on having been one of the winners. Montreal, indeed, is deeply indebted to Jacques Cartier, for it is to him that she owes her name; and I may here appropriately quote the passage in the "*Relation du Second Voyage de Jacques Cartier*," which records the fact. The whole journal affords us as a young French author lately wrote :—"*la bonne fortune de pouvoir déguster, comme un fruit d'exquise saveur, ce beau français du 16ième Siècle, un français vieux, on plutôt jeune comme l'age de Rabelais et de Montaigne, exhalanten parfum la fraicheur éternelle de l'esprit.*"

The following is the paragraph to which I refer— "*Après que nous feusmes yssus* (sortis) *de la dicte ville* (Hochelaga), *plusieurs hommes et femmes nous vinrent conduir sur la montagne cy-devant dicte, qui est par nous nommée, Mont Royal, distant du dict lieu d'ung quart de lieues. Et nous estans sur icelle montagne eusmes veue et cognaissance de plus de trente lieues à l'environ* (à l'entour) *d'icelle.*" No Montreal reader will, I am sure, be displeased if I quote, in addition, from Dr. Parkman, his picturesque description of the incident recorded by Cartier :— " A troop of Indians followed, and guided them to the top of the neighboring mountain. Cartier called it *Mont Royal*, Montreal ; and hence the name of the busy city which now holds the site of the vanished Hochelaga. Stadaconé and Hochelaga, Quebec and Montreal, in the sixteenth century as in the nineteenth, were the centres of Canadian population. From the summit, that noble prospect met his eye which at this day is the delight of tourists, but strangely changed since, first of white men, the Breton *voyageur*, gazed upon it. Tower and dome and spire, congregated roofs, white sail and gliding steamer, animate its vast expanse with varied life. Cartier saw a different scene. East, west and south, the mantling forest was over all, and the broad blue ribbon of the great river glistened amid a realm of verdure. Beyond, to the bounds of Mexico, stretched a leafy desert, and the vast hive of industry, the mighty battle-ground of later centuries, lay sunk in savage torpor, wrapped in illimitable woods."

There are two authentic portraits of Jacques Cartier; one of which is in the National Library of Paris, and the other in the City Hall of St. Malo. The former is reproduced on the title-page of " *Note sur le Manoir de Jacques Cartier*," par *M. Alfred Ramé*, (Paris, 1867), which Mr. Stephens has translated in pp. 7-9 of his " Essay ; " the latter is familiar to us all, (appearing even on bank-notes), and engravings of it will be found in Shea's editions of Le Clercq's " *Etablissement de la Foy*," and of Charlevoix's "*Histoire de la Nouvellé France* ; " in Faillon's "*Histoire de la Colonié Française*," Vol. 1; and at p. 48 of Dr. de Costa's essay on " Jacques Cartier and his Successors." This portrait might well have been taken when the gallant Commodore was gazing from Mount Royal on the unrivalled scenery by which he was surrounded. With its clear-cut features, its frank, fearless eyes and resolute chin, the noble face possesses a strange attraction for all who see it ; and we feel instinctively that the owner of that head could never have been guilty of several charges that have frequently been brought against him by writers copying their predecessors in a servile way, without due investigation, or sure warrantry of facts Full justice I believe, has never yet been done to the character of Jacques Cartier, but the charges to which I have merely referred, are gradually with the enlightening progress of research dissolving into air, like shadows at the approach of day. The latest historian of Canada seems almost to question Dr. Parkman's statement that the Breton *voyageur* was the first white man who looked forth from the top of Mount Royal. What else are we to conclude from the following words of Dr. Kingsford, except that he means to insinuate that Europeans must have visited Hochelaga previous to the time of Cartier?—" Cartier ascended the mountain, and gave it its present name of Mont Royal. Both in Montreal and Quebec he speaks of the presence of melons and cucumbers ; neither are indigenous in Canada. Cartier cannot be supposed to have misrepresented what he saw, and the fact is important. They could only have been propagated by seed ; the inference follows, by seed imported, and from Europe."

This passage reminds me that a discussion recently took place in a Montreal journal, as to whether Jacques Cartier can correctly be called " the discoverer of Canada." My opinion on the subject (*quantum valeat*), coincides with that of M. Saint Pierre, and many of the best Canadian historians, that to all intents and purposes the claims of Cartier are above those of John Cabot, who must content himself with the title of "discoverer of North America." It is not my business in this preface to argue the question, but it seems ungrateful and unjust to the French sailor to term him simply an explorer, and not the genuine " *découvreur de Canada.*" M. Saint Pierre, in the controversy referred to, well summed up the services of Jacques Cartier, and I eptomize the substance of his remarks, adapting his language to the present occasion. All that we know of the hardy Breton may be briefly stated thus :—He was probably the first of all civilized men who trod the shores of the St. Lawrence. He gave to our noble river the name it bears, and applied the Indian name of " Canada " to part of the vast territory which now forms the Dominion. He had the hardihood to trust himself with but a handful of followers in the midst of treacherous savages, over whom, however, he seemed to exercise a kind of spell. Heedless of fatigue and dangers, he travelled for hundreds of miles in a wild country, until he reached a spot where Nature bade him pause; he called the spot "Montreal," and on the very ground where he erected his tents a fair and flourishing city has since sprung up as if by magic. After his first voyage, he returned several times to Canada, and was a man of such undaunted courage, that, without hesitation, he not only faced the hardships of a Canadian winter, but in so doing, cut himself off for six months from all retreat, amid primeval forests that teemed with barbarians. During that awful winter he lost nearly half of his crews by a malignant scurvy that broke out owing to the privations they had endured. Nevertheless, his brave spirit never abandoned him. He instilled courage and hope into the hearts of the most despairing of his followers, and, after incredible sufferings, succeeded in bringing back his surviving companions to his native town of St. Malo. "Thereafter," as Dr. de Costa writes, "without having derived any material financial benefit from his great undertaking, Cartier, as the Seigneur of Limoilou, dwelt at his plain manor-house on the outskirts of St. Malo, where he died, greatly honored and respected, about the year 1555." His best epitaph may be found in his last commission, dated October 17, 1540, wherein the king of France says :—"Having confidence in the character, judgment, ability, loyalty, hardihood, great diligence, and experience of Jacques Cartier, &c."

I cannot conclude this preface without asking the reader's attention to the following words of Mr. Stephens :—"The appeal made to the public in aid of the erection of a statue to Cartier has not met with the answer it should have received; and the writer may be pardoned for confessing that his original idea in writing was to endeavor to arouse an interest in the matter and help the project." In February, 1868, a French novelist, M. Emile Chevalier, published a book with the title of "Jacques Cartier"—a book, by the way, which seems to have escaped the notice of Mr. Stephens, as it is not in his list of works connected with the subject of the essay. Here is a brief extract from M. Chevalier's book :—" *Eh ! bien*," he writes, "what I ask for Jacques Cartier, our own French Cristopher Columbus—one of those who ought to make a mark in our historic annals—one, nevertheless, of those who are least known—what I ask is a monument raised either at St. Malo, at Rennes, or even in Paris—why not ?—to transmit to posterity the memory of this great man. What I ask for the honor of my fellow countrymen, *and in the name of a million of grateful Frenchmen, who from the other side of the Atlantic will bless our work*, is that some one will put himself at the head of a movement to render to one of our most illustrious and virtuous citizens the homage which thoughtlessness, rather than ingratitude, has hitherto neglected to render to him. A statue to Jacques Cartier—to the discoverer of Canada." In 1888, a work entitled " *Une Fête de Noël sons Jacques Cartier*," by M. Ernest Myrand, was published in Quebec. It was intended by the author to be " a literary paraphrase of Jacques Cartier's second voyage," which he looks upon as undoubtedly our first historic document, since in it the discovery of Canada is related. An analysis of M. Myrand's work, from the pen of Mr. Lemoine, of Quebec, was lately printed in two consecutive numbers of the *Dominion Illustrated*. "More than twenty years," says M. Myrand, "have passed since M. Chevalier wrote—twenty years of forgetfulness, indifference and fatal silence. The book is forgotten, the enthusiasm extinguished, the dream vanished. There is no monument of Jacques Cartier anywhere in the world—no statue at St. Malo, at Rennes or in Paris! Must Cartier, then, suffer the terrible fate of sailors thus bewailed by the poet :—

*Le corps se perd dans l'eau, le nom dans la mémoire?*

This shall not be—at any rate, here in Canada, Cartier must have his share in the immortality promised by history to the memory of her heroes, and his name has not been forgotten in the province of Quebec." Here the writer drops from the cloudland of poetry, and subsides into the plainest prose, which I quote in the original French :—"*Ainsi, nous avons un collége électoral qui porte le nom de Jacques Cartier. Il y a à Montréal une place Jacques Cartier. Il existe encore, dans notre métropole commerciale, un carré Jacques Cartier, une banque Jacques Cartier, une rue Jacques Cartier. A Québec, nous avons une division municipale qui porte le nom de quartier Jacques Cartier, une marché Jacques Cartier, une rue Jacques Cartier. Nous avons encore dans le collége électoral de Québec une paroisse qui porte le nom de St. Gabriel de Val-Cartier. Puis encore, dans le même comté, le grand lac et le petit lac Jacques Cartier. Enfin, la belle et pittoresque rivière Jacques Cartier, qui donne son nom à la vallée qu'élle arrose.*

*Mais toute cette nomenclature géographique et cadastrale ne suffit pas à la renommée historique du Découvreur.*

*Aussi, l'an prochain (1889) sur la façade du Palais Legislatif, dans une des ouvertures du Campanile dédié à Jacques Cartier, le Gouvernement de la province de Quebec placera la statue, grandeur héroïque, de l'illustre Découvreur. Certes, le piédestal sera digne de l'œuvre de notre éminent artiste sculpteur Hébert, car elle dominera à cette hauteur, près de quatre cents pieds, l'estuaire de la rivière St. Charles, de cette historique rivière Cabir-Coubat qui vit dans ses eaux, le matin du 14 septembre 1535, trois petits navires pavoisés aux couleurs de France, qui portaient l'Evangile et l'avenir du Canada! L'an prochain, donc, nous aurons chez nous à Québec la statue que le patriotique écrivain Chevalier cherchait vainement sur les boulevards de St. Malo, de Rennes, et de Paris."*

Half of the year 1890 will soon be passed, and we cannot but regret with Mr. Stephens that this statue has not yet been erected. There are few men of any spirit who would not cheerfully contribute to so worthy a project; and it seems a scandal to Canada that the bold mariner who gave a name to Montreal should have no enduring monument in the province of Quebec, to record his exploits and keep his memory green. Who will take the matter in hand and enjoy the satisfaction of fulfilling, with the co-operation of all patriotic citizens, what may truthfully be regarded as almost a sacred duty and public obligation?

Poor McGee's stirring ballad of "Jacques Cartier" lies open before me; and, stimulated by the vigor of its familiar lines, I feel that if I were a man in public life, or even a man of means and leisure, I would be proud to head the desired movement, and, aided by all nationalities, carry through the project, promptly, liberally and successfully.

GEO. MURRAY.

MONTREAL, Nov. 6, 1890.

_François_

# JACQUES CARTIER.

One of the most prominent figures in Canadian history—the Columbus of Canada—is Jacques Cartier, the sturdy, courageous *voyageur* of St. Malo.

We can read of his simple courage and of his enduring faith and wisdom in the accounts of his voyages still preserved to us, and it is certain that his most striking characteristic, as thus evinced, is his strong will power and determination. His men had confidence in his judgment and trusted him— a compliment than which no higher can be paid a leader.

With regard to his life, not very much is known, apart from what is given in the Voyages, though of late years searches among the various archives have brought to light further particulars, and it is confidently believed that the Spanish and Portuguese manuscripts contain valuable details yet unpublished of this historical period.

To begin, however: The usually accepted date of Cartier's birth has hitherto been the 31st December, 1494. An "audience" held on the 23rd December, 1551, mentions "Jac Cartier, lx ans," that is sixty years of age in 1551, which would make the year of his birth 1491. Another document, just come to light, contains a statement, dated the 5th June, 1556, from Jacques Cartier, that he is sixty-four years old. In an "audience" held on the 2nd January, 1548, Jacques Cartier, in giving testimony, swears his age to be then fifty-six years. If we are to accept these official records, taken under oath, Cartier must have been born during the latter half of the year 1491, between the 7th June and the 23rd December of that year. Going back a little, it will be seen by the registers of St. Malo that Jehan Cartier was married to Guillemette Beaudoin, having six children, of whom the eldest, Jamet or Jacques, was born on the 4th December, 1458.

He married Jeffeline Jansart, and had as issue, it is now thought, the celebrated Jacques Cartier. As stated, the day of birth has usually been accepted as the 31st December, 1494, the entry being as follows: "Le xxxi jour de décembre fut baptizé un fils à Jamet Cartier et Jeffeline Jansart, sa femme et fut nommé par Guillaume Maingart, principal compère et petit compère Raoullet Perdriel." A doubt exists whether this was Jacques Cartier. There are no particulars of his life, up to the time of his marriage, worthy of mention; that is to say, it is all speculative: his early years were doubtless passed on the sea. The date of his marriage has usually been set down as taking place in 1519, and this because "avril 1519" is interlined in the register of marriages just above the entry of Jacques (Cartier) and Catherine (his wife). The year began at Easter always at St. Malo, and taking into account the fact that Easter was on the 24th April of that year, it is almost certain that the date refers to the first day of April belonging to the year 1519, according to the old style, but to 1520 according to proper notation (Longrais' "Jacques Cartier," p. 11). His wife was Catherine des Granches, daughter of Jacques des Granches, constable of the town, who was possessed of considerable property. Jacques Cartier left no issue. The name of Cartier's wife, "Katherine," occurs in the account of the "first" voyage to Canada; "first" refers to the voyage of which we have a description. That Cartier made other voyages previous to this cannot be doubted. It is stated he made three fishing voyages to Newfoundland (previous to going to Canada), and there is strong reason to suppose that he had been employed by the Portuguese to visit Brazil, about the year 1527. In the *récit* of 1545, pp. 30 and 31, reference is made to Brazil. There is also a record dated the last day of July, 1528, of the baptism of Catherine of Brazil. And Francis I. organized expeditions in 1523 and 1524 to possess himself of Brazil (Harrisse, " Revue Critique," 1876, 1er semestre, p. 20, note 3).

Before proceeding to give the accounts of the Canadian Voyages made by Cartier, I believe it advisable to give a few notes of these accounts themselves, and to state that I have translated them from, and compared them with, the originals with much care and trouble. The notes at the end of these translations, will, I think, be found of interest.

To proceed: Whether Jacques Cartier wrote the accounts of his voyages himself or not would be somewhat difficult to prove one way or the other (see note "Did Cartier," etc.), but it is certain they were written by one who took part in the expeditions. The account of the first voyage of Cartier

is to be found in Ramusio's "Collection of Voyages,"
the first edition of which was published at Venice in
1556, followed by editions in 1565, 1606 and 1613.
It appears also as "A Short and Briefe Narration of
the Two Navigations and Discoveries to the Northweaste Partes called Newe France." London, 1580.
(This was adopted by Hakluyt and followed by
Pinkerton and Churchill in their "Voyages." A
copy of it is in the Grenville collection, British
Museum.) It was published in French at Rouen in
1598 in a small octavo volume of 64 pages, under
the title, "Discours du voyage fait par le Capitaine
Jacques Cartier aux Terres-neufues de Canadas,
Norembeque, Hochelage, Labrador, et pays adjacens,
dite Nouvelle France, avec particulieres mœurs, langage et cœremonies des habitans d'icelle" (reprinted
at Paris by Tross in 1865). An account of the voyage
will also be found in Lescarbot's "Histoire de la
Nouvelle France" (livre iii., chap. ii. à v., ed. 1612),
of which there are several editions, the first appearing in 1609. "Les Archives des Voyages" de Ternaux-
Compans, 1840, also contains an account. Under the
title "Relation originale du voyage de Jacques Cartier au Canada en 1534," H. Michelaut and A. Ramé
published in 1867 an account of the first voyage from
a manuscript claimed to have been newly discovered.
There are still further the valuable publications of
the Quebec Literary and Historical Society.

As to the account of the Second Voyage, it is the
only one of which the French version is the first in
print, and of this one copy alone is known to exist,
printed at Paris in 1545 in an octavo volume of 48
pages, and now in the Grenville collection, British
Museum. (This has been reprinted in 1863 at

5

Paris.) In Lescarbot's "Histoire" the account of the Second Voyage is interpolated with an account of Champlain's doings. Lescarbot followed what is known as the Roffet text. There are also at Paris in the Bibliothèque Nationale (imperiale or royale) three manuscript accounts of the second voyage. M. Ternaux-Compans collated the two first, and published a copy in 1841, at the beginning of the second volume of the "Archives des Voyages." The Quebec Literary and Historical Society took a copy of the third manuscript, and having compared it with the two others, as well as with the account in Lescarbot, published it in 1843. The 1545 account mentioned above as having been reprinted in 1863 was collated with all three manuscripts. Lescarbot speaks of one of these manuscripts as being tied with blue silk ribbon. The Third Voyage of Cartier is related in the collection of Richard Hakluyt, of Oxford, in English, particulars of which voyage were obtained by Hakluyt during his residence in France from 1584 to 1588. They are not a complete account of the voyage. A letter from Jacques Noel, his grand-nephew, written from St. Malo on the 15th June, 1587, and a fragment of a second letter from the same source, stating that a search for further particulars had been fruitless, are given also. Hakluyt also gives Jean Allefonce's chart for 230 leagues up the St Lawrence, and an unfinished account of Roberval's voyage to the 22nd July, 1543 (?). The Quebec Literary and Historical Society published these in French in 1843. There is no account of the Fourth Voyage—if it ever took place—except in Lescarbot, who says: "He took eight months to go and get him (Roberval) after he had remained there seventeen months" (Lescarbot,

1612, p. 416) ; and " for eight months he spent in
going back to get Roberval in Canada " (Transactions Quebec Literary and Historical Society, 1862,
page 93).

une grande pipe

THE MANSION OF JACQUES CARTIER.

# THE MANOIR OF JACQUES-CARTIER.

(FROM THE ARTICLE BY M. RAMÉ.)

Captain Cartier, similarly to all the leading *bourgeois* of Saint Malo in the sixteenth century, owned in the *banlieue* of the town a "maison," of which he took his title, and where he reposed himself after his maritime expeditions. He, in fact, bears the title of "Sieur de Limoilou" in the founding of an *obit* on the 29th November, 1549, at the cathedral. This demesne of Limoilou, situated on the limits of the parishes of Parame and Saint Coulomb, a thousand metres about the hill, is a true navigator's station, established, like an observatory, at the culminating point of a hill (mamelon), which falls away on one side to Saint Ideuc, on the other to the ocean. From there, in the direction of the polar star, which had guided him on the unknown *plages* of Canada, Cartier saw Point de la Varde, not yet disfigured by the geometrical lines of a fort; to the right he had the village Roteneuf and the bay winding towards Saint Coulomb; to the left, the vast beach (*greve*) reaching or extending to the Chateau of Saint Malo; beyond all, the sea, and in the far distance the outline of Cape Frehel, a welcome mark to sailors returning to port. The manoir of Cartier remained almost entire in 1865, and its modest proportions announced not the residence of the man who had given the King of France a kingdom larger than France itself. The penury shown in faulty construction and poor building materials proved that the captain had gained more fame than money in his adventurous voyages. The buildings were placed on two sides of a square yard, enclosed for the rest by high walls. Knowing the fury of the west and north winds on the Brittany coast, Cartier had placed his living room upstairs, and had only one story *sur rez de chaussée*. Each floor had two rooms ; the lower a kitchen and a *salle*, the upper a *reduit* and the chamber of the captain. The stairway, contained or placed in a round tower, abutted forth (*faisait saillie*) on the yard, and relieved the monotony of the façade. The wall of the east looked on the garden. To that of the west was attached a lower building used as a horse stable. In front, on the opposite side of the yard, was the barn, the *pressoir* and the cow stable. In the centre of the yard was a large square well, with a fine finish of granite, yielding plenty of water. Entrance was made into the yard by a large door (*charretière*), without any ornament except a shield held by two angels, in a prominent position. The field of the shield was simply an open quarter. They were " speaking arms." This sculpture in granite *très fineste* is reproduced :—

(En guise de fleur or) 0m. 45 high.
0m. 55 wide.

It is not to be believed, as a print would lead us to believe (which print is in the St. Malo museum, and which has been reprinted by a Nantes litho- . grapher), that this gateway was furnished with a double door with columns, one destined for foot travelers, the other for vehicles; nor is it to be believed that the date of 1545 was cut on the keystone. All these are imaginings of the *dessinateur*, who, finding the gateway too modest, constructed one in his picture, and one belonging to a later period. He gives the shield and two angels a height of six feet. These might be the Cartier letters of nobility, which were granted him, it is said, by Francis I.; he did not exaggerate at this point the dimension of these *insignes nobiliares*. This shield proves further, besides the fact of the ennobling, if it be true, that Jacques Cartier did not belong to those Cartiers, *sieurs du Hindret et de la Boulaye*, who had arms of blue and silver with four blies on each and who were ennobled between 1478 and 1513.

It could be denied that all the buildings of the manoir go back to the time of Cartier. Thus, the form of the openings of the *logis*, the mouldings of the woodwork of the doors and windows appear in part more modern than the sixteenth century, though the *souche de l'edifice* belongs to the primitive plan. It is necessary to say as much of the frames of painted glass which *garnissant* (adorn) the windows of the principal room to the east. These frames represent in the centre, in a circular medallion, St. Bertrand and St. Julien, and round these, in small square divisions, landscape., a fox hunting scene, trees, a chateau, a fountain, etc. These are treated in the manner of the end of the seventeenth century, and in a manner negligent. They are, as a whole, very mediocre works, and it is impossible to consider them in any way as souvenirs.

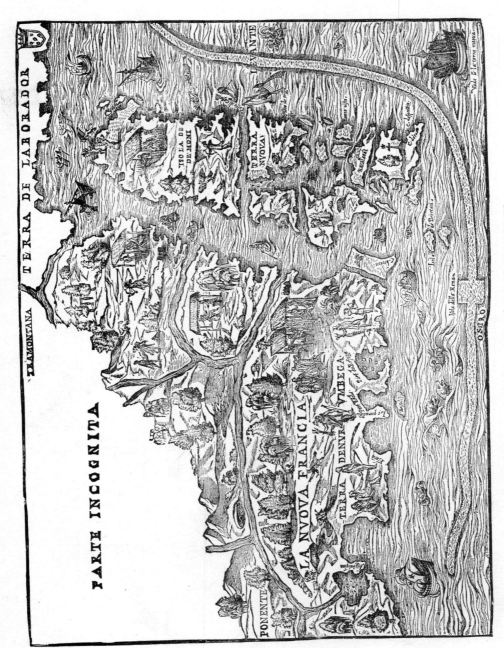

GASTALDIS' MAP—REDUCED FROM ONE IN RAMUSIO.

# FIRST VOYAGE.

In Ramusio, edition, 1556.  Vol. iii., page 435.

A Shorte and Briefe Narration of the Two Navigations and Discoveries to the Northweaste Partes called Newe France, London, 1580.  Hakluyt adopted this in his edition of 1600, and it has been followed by Pinkerton and Churchill in their voyages.

Discours du Capitaine Jacques Cartier aux Terres Neuves du Canada, Norembeque, Hochelage, Labrador, et pays adjacens dite Nouvelle France, avec particulierès mœurs, langage et cérémonies des habitans d'icelle.  Rouen, 1598.  Chez Raphael du Petit-Val. Octavo, 64 p.

In Lescarbot, edition 1612.  Lib. iii., chap. 2, page 240, *et seq.*

Relation Originale du Voyage de Jacques Cartier au Canada en 1534; Documents inédits sur Jacques Cartier et le Canada (nouvelle série) publiés par H. Michelaut et A. Ramé, accompagnés de deux portraits de Cartier et de deux vues de son manoir.  Paris, Tross, 1867.

*How Sir Charles de Moüy of La Mailleraye sent away two ships of St. Malo to the New Land of France, and how they reached the Harbor of Cape Bonne-Veue.*

After Sir Charles de Moüy of La Mailleraye and Vice-Admiral of France had sworn the captains, mates and sailors of the ships to be well and faithfully true to the service of His Christian Majesty the King, under the authority and charge of Jacques Cartier, we set sail, the twentieth of April, 1534, from St. Malo, with two ships, each about sixty tons, and manned with sixty-one men each ; we had such good weather that on the tenth of May we arrived at Newfoundland, into which we entered by the Cape de Bonne-Veue, which is in latitude 48½° and longitude * * On account of the large quantity of ice along the coast here, we were obliged to enter a harbor we named St. Catherine, distant about five leagues to the south-southeast. Here we stayed ten days waiting for favorable weather, and during this time we fitted up and got ready our boats.

*How we arrived at the Island of Birds, and the large numbers of birds found there.*

The twenty-first of May we set sail with a westerly wind and went north from Cape de Bonne-Veue to Isle des Oiseaux (Bird Island), which was completely surrounded with ice, broken in pieces ; in spite of the ice our boats went there to get birds, which are present in incredible numbers as to seem to have been *brought* and *sown* (*sic*) expressly on the island, which is about a league in circuit. The birds are, however, a hundred times more abundant around the island, in the air and on the water ; some are as large as magpies, black and white, and with the beak of ravens ; they are always on the water, being unable to fly high, as their wings are small, not larger than half a hand, with which wings, however, they fly on the surface of the water, as other birds do in the air. They are very fat, and are called by the natives *apporrath.* Our two boats were filled with them in less than half an hour, as quickly as if we had been loading stones, so that on each ship we salted four or five casks full, without those we ate fresh.

*Of the two species of birds, one called Godetz, the other Mar-*
*gaulx, and our arrival at Carpunt.*

There is besides another kind of bird, which flies
high in the air and on the surface of the water,
smaller than the others, and is called godetz. They
gather on this island and hide themselves under the
wings of the large birds. There is another sort,
larger and white, staying in another district of the
island ; these are difficult of capture, as they bite like
dogs ; they call them Margaux. Though this island
is distant fourteen leagues from the mainland, yet
bears come there to eat the birds, and our men found
one as big as a cow, white as a swan, which jumped
into the water before them. Next day, Easter, as we
were sailing towards the mainland, we met with
this bear, swimming in the same direction as rapidly
as we sailed ; we gave chase in our boats and took
him by main force ; his flesh was as delicate as that
of a two-year old heifer. On Wednesday following
we arrived at Castle Gulf (Straits of Belle-Isle), but
on account of bad weather and the large quantities
of ice, we found it necessary to go to a harbor near
by, called Carpunt, whence we were unable to come
out till the ninth of June, when we set sail to go
beyond Carpunt, which is in latitude 51°.

*Description of the new land from Cape Race to Cape Degrad.*

The district from Cape Race to Cape Degrad forms
the point of entry to the said gulf, which latter
looks from cape to cape, to the east, north and south.
All this part is full of islands, one after the other,
between which there are small channels, by which
one can go and come in small boats, and there are

also good harbors like Carpunt and Degrad. From the highest of these islands can be seen clearly, by any one standing, the two low-lying islands near Cape Race, from which place it is twenty-five leagues to the port of Carpunt, and there are two channels, one on the east side, the other on the south, but it is necessary to beware of the east channel, as there are reefs and shallows, and it is necessary to go around the island to the west, half a cable's length or a little less, then turn south towards Carpunt, and be watchful of three reefs under the water and in the channel ; towards the island, on the east side, there is a depth of three or four fathoms and good bottom. The other entrance looks to the east and on the west one can land.

*Of the Island named St. Catherine.*

Leaving Point Degrad, at the entrance of the said gulf going west, care must be taken regarding two islands on the right, one of which is distant three leagues from this point, and the other seven leagues, more or less, from the first ; low and flat, and apparently part of the mainland. I named this island St. Catherine, in the eastern portion of which is a dry and sterile region of about a quarter of a league, to reach which it is necessary to make a little circuit. In this island is Castle Harbor, which looks (lies) north-northeast and south-southwest, and the distance from one to the other is about fifteen leagues. From Castle Harbor to the Port des Gouttes, which is the district north of the gulf already spoken of, which lies east-northeast and west-southwest, the distance is twelve leagues and a half, and is distant two leagues from Port des Balances, and a third part of this crossing is thirty fathoms deep. From Port des Balances to Blanc Sablon (White Sand) is twenty-five leagues to the west-southwest. It is well to give warning that to the southwest of Blanc Sablon there is a reef three leagues long appearing above the water and resembling a boat.

*Of Blanc Sablon, Isle of Brest, Bird Island; the kind and number of birds found there, and of the Port des Ilettes.*

Blanc Sablon is a place having no shelter from the south or southwest, but south-southwest of it are two islands, one called Isle of Brest, the other Bird Island (Isle des Oiseaux), on which are a large number of godetz and ravens with red beaks and red feet, which make their nests underground, like rabbits. Passing a cape a league from Blanc Sablon are found a harbor and channel named Les Ilettes, which is the best place of Blanc Sablon, and where there are excellent fishing grounds. From Les Ilettes to Port Brest the distance is about eighteen leagues around, and this port is in latitude 51° 55′ and longitude    *    *    Between Les Ilettes and this latter place are several islands, and Port Brest is itself amidst islands which surround it for more than three leagues, and these islands are so flat and low-lying that the mainland can be seen over them.

*How we went into Port Brest with the ships, and going further west passed amongst Les Ilettes and found them so innumerable as to defy counting; we named them The Islands.*

On the 10th of June, we went into Port Brest with our ships to procure wood and water and get ready to go beyond the gulf. On the day of Saint Barnabé, after hearing mass, we went with the boats outside this port to the west to discover others, and we went among the islands which are so numerous that it is impossible to count them, because they are found for ten leagues from Port Brest. We stopped on one of the islands to pass the night, and found a very large number of ducks' eggs and those of other birds which nest here. We named them all The Islands.

*Of Ports Saint Antoine, Saint Servan, Jacques Cartier, the river St. James; of the garb and costumes of the natives of the island of Blanc Sablon.*

Next day we passed beyond these islands, and at the end of a multitude of them found a good harbor, which we named Port Saint Antoine, and beyond this we discovered, to the southwest, a small river, which is very deep, between two other districts, and there is a good harbor here. We erected a cross here, and named the harbor Port Saint Servan; and southwest of this place and river, about a league distant, is a small island, round-shaped like an oven, surrounded with many other small ones, which are a mark or means of knowing these harbors. Two leagues further there is another fine stream, and larger, in which we caught many salmon, and named it River St. James. In this river we met with a large ship from La Rochelle, which had passed the night before beyond Port Brest, where they desired to fish, but the seamen did not know where it was. We went by the side of them and sailed together to another port, further to the west, about a league from the River St. James, which I believe to be one of the best harbors in the world, and which we named Port Jacques Cartier. If the land corresponded in value to the harbors, it would be a benefit, but it does not deserve the name of Newfoundland, consisting merely of stones and wild rocks suitable for wild animals only ; and in all the northern part I did not see enough soil to fill a cart, though I went ashore in several places. On the island of Blanc Sablon there is nothing but moss and small thorn bushes, dry and half dead ; in fact, I think this is the land that God gave to Cain. Here are men of fine shape and stature, but indomitable and savage. They wear their hair tied on the top of their heads like a bunch of hay, passing through it a small piece of wood, or something similar, in place of a nail (pin), and they also attach there some bird's feathers. They wear skins, men and women, the latter being completely covered and girded at the waist (which the men are not) ; they paint themselves with certain red colors. They make their boats of the bark of the boul tree, and take large quantities of seals. And since I came there I learned that this was not their place of habitation, but that they come by land from a warmer country to secure the seals and other things necessary for their subsistence.

*Of other capes: Cape Double, Cape Pointu, Cape Royal, Cape Milk; Hut Mountains, and Pigeon-house Islands.*

On the thirteenth we returned with our boats to the ships to sail, as the weather was favorable ; Sunday we heard mass ; Monday following, the fifteenth, we passed outside Port Brest and made our way southwards to examine land we had seen, and which seemed to be two islands ; but, when we

2

were about the middle of the gulf, we perceived it
to be the mainland, and there was a cape here which
was double, one above the other, for which reason
we named it Cape Double. At the beginning of
the gulf we took a sounding, and found a hundred
fathoms on all sides. From Port Brest to Cape
Double the distance is about twenty leagues, and
five or six leagues from there we took another
sounding and found forty fathoms. This land looks
northeast-southwest. Next day, the sixteenth, we
sailed along the coast southwest-a-quarter-south,
thirty-five leagues from Cape Double, and found very
high and rocky mountains, amongst which we saw
some small huts (*cabannes*), so we called them Hut
Mountains; the other lands and mountains are very
irregular and broken, and between them and the
sea the land is low. The day previous, owing to
the fog and dimness, we had seen no land, but in
the evening we perceived an opening in the land
which appeared to be the mouth of a river, amongst
these Hut Mountains; and to the southwest of us,
about three leagues, was a cape without any peak
or point all round the top of it, but jutting out into
a point at its base; it received the name of Cape
Pointed. North of this cape is a flat island, and as
we wished to explore this entrance (*embouchure*) to
see if there was a good harbor, we lowered sails to
pass the night here. Next day, the seventeenth,
we had wind from the northwest, and were obliged
to leave the cape and make our way southwest
till Thursday morning, sailing about thirty-seven
leagues, and found ourselves among several islands
shaped like pigeon-houses (dove-cots), so they were
named Pigeon-house Islands.

Lescarbot here has the following interpolation :—
Gulf St. Julien is distant seven leagues from Cape
Royal, which is situated to the south-one-quarter
southwest. South-southwest of this cape is another
cape, all cleft underneath and round in shape on the
summit. On the north is a small island half a
league distant, and this cape was called Milk Cape.
Between these two capes there are certain low lands
which appear to have streams. Two leagues from
Cape Royal the depth of water is twenty fathoms,
and there is excellent cod fishing here ; we took
more than a hundred in less than an hour, while
waiting.

*Of some islands between Cape Royal and Cape Milk.*

Next day, the eighteenth, the wind became so
contrary and violent that we felt obliged to return
towards Cape Royal, thinking to find a safe harbor ;
and with our boats we went to see what there was
between Cape Royal and Cape Milk. Beyond the
low lands was a very deep gulf, in which there are
several islands ; this gulf is shut in on the south
side. The low lands form one side of the entrance
and Cape Royal is on the other side, and the low
lands run out into the sea more than half a league.
The district is flat and sterile (bad land) ; in the
middle of the entrance is an island. This gulf is in
latitude 48½°, and in longitude * *  We found no
harbor this day, and on account of nightfall returned
out to sea, turning the cape to the west.

*Of the Island St. John.*

From this day to the twenty-fourth of the month,
the feast of St. John, we were tempest-tossed, and

had such bad winds and dark weather that we saw no land till St. John's day, when we discovered a cape lying to the southwest of Cape Royal, distant thirty-five leagues; but the mist was so heavy and the weather so bad this day that we could not land. And as this was the day of St. John, the cape was named St. John.

*Of the islands called the Islands of Margaulx; the birds and animals found there. Of the Island Brion and Cape Dauphin.*

Next day, the twenty-fifth, the weather was still very unfavorable; we sailed part of the day to the west and northwest, and in the evening we went across up to the time of the second watch since we had left, and then we ascertained by our quadrant that we were heading northwest-a-quarter-west, distant seven leagues and a half from Cape St. John; and when we wished to sail on, the wind changed to the northwest, so that we ran to the south fifteen leagues, and came to three islands, of which two had coasts perpendicular like a wall, so that it was impossible to ascend them; between them is a small reef. These islands were more completely filled (covered) with birds than a field is with grass, which birds nest here. On the largest island was a large number of birds that we called margaulx, which are white and larger than a goose (gosling); these frequent one portion of the island, and on the other portion were the kind called godetz; but on the banks were the godetz and large apporrath, resembling those mentioned before. We went on the lower side of the smallest island, and gathered more than a thousand godetz and apporrath, and loaded our boats with as many as we wished, and could have filled thirty boats in an hour. These islands received the name of Margaulx Islands. Five leagues to the west from here is another island, two leagues long and two wide; here we stopped for the night to procure wood and water. It is surrounded with sand, and there is a depth of six or seven fathoms. These islands were of the best soil we had yet seen; in fact, one field here is worth the whole of Newfoundland. Full of large trees are these islands; of fields of wild wheat, and of peas as fine as in Brittany, which seemed to have been sown by hand; there were also barberries, strawberries, red roses, grapes, and many sweet flowers and grasses. There are large animals about this island, as large as an ox, having tusks like an elephant, and which live in the sea. We saw one sleeping on the water's edge, and went towards it with our boat, thinking to secure it, but as soon as it heard us it threw itself in the water. We saw bears and wolves also. This island was named Isle of Brion; around it on the southeast and northwest are large marshes. I think, from what I could make out, that there is a channel between the New Land and the Island of Brion. If this should be so, it would shorten the time and journey, provided it could be done by this route. Four leagues west-southwest from this island is the mainland, which resembles an island surrounded with small islands of sand. There there is a fine cape, which we named Cape Dauphin, because it is the commencement of good lands. The twenty-seventh of June we made a circuit of the lands lying west-southwest, which appear from a distance to be hills or mountains of sand, though they are low lands and of little depth. We could not approach them, much less effect a landing, on account of the contrary wind. This day we made fifteen leagues.

*Of the island called Alezay and Cape St. Peter.*

The next day we coasted along these shores ten leagues to a cape of red earth, which is rough and indented, through an opening or cleft in which may be seen a low country to the north; and there is a lowland between a sheet of water and the ocean. From this cape and sheet of water to another cape is about fourteen leagues, and is shaped in a semicircle, consisting of sand like a ditch, over which can be seen marshes and sheets of water as far as the eye can see. Before arriving at the first cape there are two islands quite near shore. Five leagues from the second cape is an island to the southwest which is very high and peaked; this latter we named Alezay; the former cape we named Cape St. Peter, as it was on his day we arrived there.

*Of the Cape Orleans. Of the Canoe River (barques). Of Cape of the Savages; the nature and temperature of the country.*

From Brion island to this place there is a good sandy bottom, and having taken soundings also to the southwest up to five leagues of the land, we found twenty-five fathoms; a league nearer, twelve fathoms; and near shore six fathoms, more or less, and good bottom. But as we wished to have more knowledge of these rocky bottoms, full of stones, we lowered the sails. Next day, the last but one of the month, the wind came from the south-one-quarter-southwest; we sailed west until Tuesday morning, the last of the month, without discovering any other

land, with the exception that in the evening we saw
some land, apparently forming two islands, lying
behind us nine or ten leagues to the west and southwest. This day, till sunrise next morning, we made
about forty leagues. We thought the land appearing like two islands was the mainland, situated to
the southwest and north-northeast, up to a beautiful
cape called Cape Orleans. All this land is low and
flat, and as fine as one can see anywhere, full of fine
trees and prairies; but we could find no harbor, as
there is nothing but reefs and sand-bars. We went
several times with our boats, and, amongst other
places, we entered a fine stream of little depth, for
which reason it was named Canoe River. We saw
several canoes with savages crossing the river, but
held no intercourse with them, because the wind
came from the sea and blew on shore, so that we
returned to the ships. We sailed northeast till sunrise next day, the first of July, when a violent tem-
pest arose, so that we had to lower the sails till
about two hours before noon, when it cleared off,
and we perceived Cape Orleans and another seven
leagues distant to the north-a-quarter-northeast,
which was named Cape of the Savages. Northeast
of this cape about half a league there is a very dangerous rocky reef. While near this cape we perceived a man who ran behind our boats as we
coasted along, and made signs to us that we ought
to return to the cape. Seeing his signs, we began
to go towards him, when, seeing us come, he took
flight. Landing, we placed before him a knife and
a woollen waistband on a stick. We returned to
our ships. This day we went along this coast, turning and winding nine or ten leagues, without find-

ing a good harbor, as all this country is low and full
of reefs and sand bars. Notwithstanding which,
this day we went on shore in four places to see the
trees, which are beautiful here and very odorous;
there are cedars, yews, pine, white elms, ash, willows, and others unknown to us, but all without
fruit. The land, where there are no trees, is very
fertile and full of peas, of white and red barberries,
of strawberries, of wild wheat, like rye, which seems
to have been sown and cultivated. And the temperature here is as favorable as one could wish, and very
warm; there are many thrushes, wood-pigeons and
other birds; in fact, nothing is lacking except good
harbors.

*Of Gulf St. Lunaire and other noteworthy gulfs and capes; the
nature and fertility of the soil.*

Next day, the second of July, we came to and
explored the land of the north coast opposite us,
which joins that already spoken of; having made
the circuit, we found that it contained * * * of
width and the same diameter. We named it Gulf
St. Lunaire. We went to the cape on the north with
our boats, and found the land so low that for a
league there was not more than a fathom of water.
Seven or eight leagues northeast of this cape is another cape to the north, between which is a triangular
gulf (bay), very deep and running far up into the
land; it lies to the northeast. This gulf is surrounded with bars and shallows for ten leagues;
there are not more than two fathoms of water. It is
fifteen leagues between the two capes. Beyond
these we saw a land and a cape, which lies north-
a-quarter-northeast as far as we could see. All

night it was stormy and wild ; so much so that we were obliged to carry reefed sails till next morning, the third of July, when the wind blew from the west, and we were carried north, and discovered the land which was north-northeast of the low lands. Between these low lands and the high lands is a large gulf and opening, of fifty-five fathoms in many places and about fifteen leagues wide. On account of the depth, size and character of the land here, we had hopes of finding a passage similar to that of Castle Gulf. This gulf looks east-northeast, west-southwest. The soil on the south side is good enough and cultivable, and full of as fine prairies as we had seen, level as a lake ; on the north side are high mountains, covered with trees of various kinds, amongst others fine cedars and firs fit to make masts for vessels of three hundred tons ; and we saw no part here that was not covered with these woods, except two places where it was low ; these were fine prairies, with two beautiful lakes. The centre of this gulf is in latitude 47½°.

*Of Cape Hope. Of Bay (staria) St. Martin ; how seven canoes of the savages came to our boat, and being unwilling to go away, we frightened them by firing small cannon, so that they fled in great haste.*

The cape of this land to the south was named Cape Hope, by reason of the hope we had of finding a passage. The fourth of July we went along this coast northwards to find a harbor, and went into a small place exposed to the south wind, which we thought it worth while to name St. Martin, and we stayed here from the fourth till the twelfth. While here we went with one of our boats on Monday, the sixth, the Feast of the Mass, after hearing Mass, to explore a cape and point of land seven or eight leagues from the west coast; to see also which way the land lies. Having come within about a half league of the point, we perceived two groups (bands) of canoes of savages going from one side to the other; and there were more than forty or fifty canoes, of which a portion reached the point and jumped ashore, with a great deal of noise, making signs to us to land, showing us skins on pieces of wood. But as we had only one boat, we were unwilling to do so, and went towards the others who were on the water. The others, seeing us fleeing, ordered two of their largest canoes to follow us, with which were gathered five of those coming from the ocean, and the seven approached our boat, making signs of joy and showing a desire for friendship, saying in their language, "*Napen tondamen assurtah,*" and other unintelligible words. But as has been said we had only one boat and did not care to trust in their signs, and made them signs to go away from us, which they would not do, and came with great ado to us, so that our boat was soon surrounded with their seven canoes. And because our signs to them to retire had no effect, we fired off two small cannons over them; this astonishing them, they went back towards the point, stayed there awhile, then again began to come near us as before; so that, when near our boat, we shot two of our darts amongst them, which frightened them so much that they fled in great haste and were not willing to return.

*Our traffic with the savages.*

The next day some of the savages came in their canoes to the point and mouth of the bay whence our ships had gone. Knowing of their having come, we went with our boat where they were, but as soon as they saw us coming they fled, making signs they had come to trade with us, showing the skins of little value, which they wore. We likewise made them signs that we wished them no harm ; and two of our men went ashore to go to them, taking knives and other iron tools, also a red cap to present to their captain. Seeing this, they landed and brought skins and began trading, showing great excitement and joy at possessing the knives and iron tools, dancing and performing antics, such as throwing themselves in the water on their heads with their hands. They gave us all they had, retaining nothing; so that they were obliged to go away perfectly naked. They made signs to us they would return next day, bringing other skins.

*How some of the men went ashore with articles of trade and three hundred savages came, who were overjoyed ; of the nature of the country, its products and the gulf called the Gulf (Bay) of Chaleur.*

Thursday, the eighth of the month, as the wind was not favorable for us to go out with our ships, we got ready our boats to explore the gulf and made about twenty-five leagues this day. Next day, having good weather, we sailed till noon, when we had explored the greater part of the gulf and saw that beyond the low lands there was a high mountainous district. But, as we perceived there was no

passage, we coasted along, and as we sailed saw
some savages on the shores of a lake in the low lands,
making several fires. We went there and found
there was a channel from the sea into the lake, and
we placed our boats on one of the banks of the
channel. The savages approached us and brought
us pieces of cooked seal, which they placed on pieces
of wood and then retired, giving us to understand
that they gave them to us. We sent men ashore with
hatchets, knives, chaplets, and other articles, in
which the savages took great delight, and they came
all at once in their canoes to the shore where we
were, bringing skins and other things they had to
exchange for our articles, and there were more than
three hundred of them—men, women and children.
A number of the women had stopped, remaining in
the water to their knees, dancing and singing. Others,
who had come to where we were, came familiarly
rubbing our arms with their hands, then raised
towards heaven and danced and made signs of joy;
and had so much confidence, that finally they ex-
changed everything they had; so that they found
themselves stark naked, as they had given up all
they had, which was of little value. We perceived
that these people could be easily converted to our
Faith. They go from one place to another, living by
fishing; their country is warmer than Spain, as fine
a country as one would wish to see, level and smooth,
and there is no part too small for trees, even if sandy,
or where there is no wild wheat, which has an ear
like that of rye and the grains like oats; there are peas
as thick as if sown and cultivated, red and white
barberries, strawberries, red and white roses, and
other flowers of sweet and delightful perfume. There

are also fine prairies, fine grasses and lakes filled
with salmon. They call a hatchet in their language
"cochi," and a knife "bacon." We named this gulf
the Gulf of Chaleur.

*Of another tribe (natione) of savages, their customs, food and
dress.*

Being certain there was no passage by way of this
gulf, we set sail from St. Martin on Sunday, the 12th,
to explore further. We went eastward along the
coast about eighteen leagues as far as Capo di Prato,
where we found it shallow and a very high tide,
very rough water, so that we went towards land
between the cape and an island to the east about a
league from the cape, and there we anchored for the
night. Next morning we set sail to follow along this
coast, which runs north-northeast, but a furious gale
sprang up and we had to return to our anchoring
place, where we stayed till next day, when we again
set sail and came to a river five or six leagues from
Capo di Prato; having crossed the river, the wind
again became violent, and there was such a heavy fog
that we had to go within the river on Wednesday,
the 14th, and we stayed here till the 16th awaiting
favorable weather. On Friday, the 16th, the wind
blew such a gale that one of the ships lost an anchor,
and we were obliged to go seven or eight leagues
to a harbor with good bottom, which we had discovered with our boats, and the bad weather kept
us here till the 25th. Meanwhile we saw a large
number of savages, who were mackerel fishing,
which are very plentiful; there were about forty
canoes of them, and more than two hundred men,
women and children, who, after meeting us on shore,

came familiarly (freely) to our ships with their
canoes. We gave them knives, glass chaplets
(beads), combs and other articles of little value,
which greatly pleased them; they lifted their hands
to heaven as they sang and danced in their canoes.
They can with truth be called savages, as there are
no people poorer than these in the world, and I
believe they do not possess anything to the value of
five pennies, apart from their canoes and nets.
Their whole clothing consists of a small skin, with
which they cover their loins (le parti vergognose);
they also put other old skins above and across their
bodies. They have not the same nature (character,
disposition), nor language as the first ones we had
seen. They have their heads completely shaven,
except a lock of hair on the top of the head which
they allow to grow as long as a horse's tail; they tie
it to their heads with small leather cords. Their
dwellings are their canoes, which they turn upside
down and lie down under them on the bare ground.
They eat their meat almost raw, merely warming
it over coals; the same with fish. We went, the
Day of the Magdalen, with our boats where they
were, and landed freely amongst them, which
pleased them, and all the men danced and sang in
two or three bands (groups), making great signs of
joy at our coming. They had sent away into the
forest all the young women except two or three who
had remained with them, to each one of whom we
gave a comb and a tin bell, which pleased them, and
they rubbed the arms and chest of our captain, as they
thanked him. The savages, noticing we had given
presents to the women who remained, caused the
others to come out of the forest, so that they might

also receive some as well as the others. There were about twenty women who threw themselves in a heap on our captain, touching and stroking him, their method of caressing. He gave each of them a tin bell of little value, and they immediately began to dance, singing several songs. We found here a large quantity of mackerel that they had caught near this shore with nets made expressly for the purpose of the fibre of hemp, which grows in the district where they usually live : they do not go to sea except when it is favorable for fishing, as I have been informed. Likewise there grows also in the same district a kind of grain large as peas, similar to what grows in Spain ; this they eat in place of bread ; they have an abundance of it ; they call it in their language *Kapaige.* They have also plums, which they dry as we do for the winter ; they call them *Honesta.* They have figs also, nuts, apples and other fruits, and beans which they call *Sahu ;* the nuts, *Cahehya ;* figs. * * * ; apples, * * * If we showed them an article they did not have and did not know what it was, shaking their heads, they would reply *Nohda,* which means they have none and do not know what it is. They showed us by signs how they prepared the things (foods, etc.), they have and how they grow. They will not eat anything that is salted ; are great thieves and steal all they can.

*How we erected a large cross on the point at the entrance to the harbor, and the chief of the savages made a long speech. Our captain secured two of the chief's sons to go with us.*

On the twenty-fourth we made a large cross, thirty feet high ; this was made in the presence of some of the savages at the point at the entrance of the harbor, on the middle of which cross we put a shield (escutcheon) in relief with three fleur-de-lys, above which was cut in large letters:

"VIVE LE ROY DE FRANCE,"

and we erected it in their presence on the point, and they looked at it keenly, both when we were making it and while erecting it. Having erected it we all joined hands and knelt down in adoration of it before their eyes, and we made signs to them, looking and pointing to heaven, that in this was our salvation. This astonished them greatly; they turned to each other and looked at the cross. Having gone back to our ships, their captain (chief) came to us in a canoe, wearing an old black bearskin, with his three daughters and his brother; they did not come as close as usual. The chief made a long speech, pointing to the cross and making a representation of it with his two fingers. Then he pointed to the district round us, as if to say it was all his, and that we should not have erected the cross without his permission. Having finished we showed him a ring or hatchet (*manara*), as if we wished to exchange it for his bearskin, which attracted him, and he gradually came close to our ships. One of our sailors who was in the ship's boat laid his hand on the canoe, and instantly jumped into it with two or three more, and obliged them to go on board ship, at which they were much astonished. But our captain at once assured them they would receive no hurt, making signs of friendship to them, welcoming them to eat and drink. After this, we gave them to understand by signs that the cross was placed there as a guide and mark to enter the harbor, and that we wished to return here shortly and that we would bring iron tools and other things, and that we wished to take with us two of his sons and that we would return again to this harbor. And we dressed each of the sons in a shift, a colored sack (waist), and a red capo, and we placed a brass chain around the neck of each, which pleased them immensely. They gave their old clothes (?) to those who returned. We gave a hatchet and some knives to each one of the three we sent back; these having reached shore and related what had passed to the others, about noon-time six of their canoes, with five or six men in each, came to the ships, bringing fish to the chief's daughters and bid them adieu, and said some words to them which we could not understand. They made signs that they would not remove the cross.

*How we left the harbor, making our way ahead, and leaving this coast behind us, we set out for a land west-northwest.*

Next day, the twenty-fifth, there was a good wind, and we left the above harbor. Being outside, we sailed to east-northeast, seeing that near the estuary of this river, land is round in shape and forms a gulf in the shape of a half-circle; so that from our ships we saw the whole coast, leaving which behind us we set out for a land to the west-northwest; there was another gulf (bay) twenty leagues from the river we had just left.

*Of Capes St. Louis and Montmorenci (Memoransi) and some other lands; and how one of our boats struck a reef and stopped us from going further.*

Monday, the twenty-seventh, at sunset we coasted along this land, which lies southeast and northwest, and on Wednesday we saw another cape where the land begins to turn eastward. We coasted fifteen leagues, and here the land turns towards the north; at three leagues from the cape there is a depth of twenty-four fathoms. These lands here are flat, and with less wood than any we had yet seen. There are fine green prairies and stretches of country. This cape was named St. Louis, being the day of that saint; it is in latitude 49½° and longitude * * This day (Wednesday), in the morning, we were east of the cape, and we went northwest to approach the land, at nightfall, and found that it looked north and south. Between Cape St. Louis and another named Montmorenci, fifteen leagues distant, the land begins to turn to the northwest. We wished to take soundings three leagues from this cape, and could not find bottom with one hundred and fifty fathoms. We sailed about ten leagues further along this coast to latitude 50°. The Saturday following, the first of August, at sunrise, we came to other lands on the north and northeast, which were high and serrated, apparently mountains, between which there were other low lands with woods and rivers. We sailed about these lands, heading northwest, to see if there was a gulf or passage, till the fifth of the month. The distance between these lands is fifteen leagues, and the centre of them is in latitude 50° 20', and we had great difficulty to make more than five leagues, by reason of the strong tides and violent winds prevalent there. We did not go further than five leagues, whence we could see the land on one side and the other, and here it begins to widen. But as we were at the mercy of the wind, we went south, endeavoring to reach a cape to the south,

which was the furthest out in the sea of any we
could find, and distant from us about fifteen leagues.
But having come near it we found it to be rocks,
reefs and bars, which we had not found in parts to
the south, from Cape St. John; the tide carried us to
the westward against the wind, so that, following
the coast one of our boats stuck on a reef and could
go no further, so we had to get out to float it off.

*Having consulted together as to the most advisable thing to do,
we (they) determine to turn ; of the straits called St. Pierre
and Cape Tiennot.*

Having proceeded along the coast about two hours,
the tide became so strong that we could make no
headway against it with thirteen oars, further than a
stone's throw. So that we got out of our boats,
leaving some to watch them, and ten or twelve of us
proceeded on shore to the cape, where we found
that the land turns to the southwest. Having seen
this, we returned to our boats, went back to the
ships, which had sails set with the hope of proceeding further ; but they had been beaten back by the
wind four leagues from where we had left them.
Having reached them, we held a council of the captains, sailors, mates and the rest to decide what was
most expedient for us to do. After each one had
spoken, we saw that the east winds were becoming
very violent and that the sea was running so high
that we were beaten back, and that it was impossible to accomplish anything ; also that tempests
(storms) are frequent at this season in Newfoundland ; that we were in a distant country, did not
know the risks and dangers of the return voyage,
and also that we had either to return at once or

remain the rest of the year. Besides which it was
stated that if the wind changed to the north we
would be unable to leave at all. Having considered
these points, we made up our minds to return. And
as it was on St. Peter's day we came into this strait,
we named it St. Peter's Straits (Belle Isle). We took
soundings in several parts of it and found one hundred fathoms, and one hundred and fifty fathoms,
and near shore sixty fathoms. From this day till
Wednesday we had a favoring wind, and we coasted
north, east-southeast, west and northwest, for such
is its configuration, except along a cape of some low
land which turns more to the south, distant about
twenty-five leagues from the straits. Here we saw
smoke caused by the people of the country above the
cape, but as the wind was not favorable to go inshore,
we did not do so. Seeing that we did not approach
them, twelve of them came to us in two canoes,
and came alongside as freely as if they had been of
our own people, telling us they came from the Grand
Gulf, and that their captain (chief) was named
Tiennot ; the latter was on the cape making signs to
them to return to their country (which we had left).
They had a large quantity of fish. We named it
Cape Tiennot. Beyond this cape all the land lies
south-southeast, west-northwest ; it is low, fertile,
surrounded with sand near the sea; there are
marshes and shallows for about twenty leagues
along here, after which the land turns from the
west to the east and northeast, and is completely
surrounded with islands two or three leagues from
shore. And it appeared to us that there were several
dangerous reefs four or five leagues from land.

*How on the ninth of August we came within Blanc Sablon, and
the fifth September arrived at St. Malo.*

From Wednesday till Saturday we had a strong
wind from the southwest, which made us point east-
northeast, on which latter day we reached the district
in the eastern part of New Land between Hut Mountains and Cape Double. Here an east wind blew
with great violence; therefore, we put the cape
northeast by north, to approach the north coast,
which is, as has been said, completely surrounded
with islands. Being near these, the wind changed
to the south and took us into the gulf so quickly that
by the grace of God we came next day, the ninth of
August, within Blanc Sablon, which is all we have
discovered. The fifteenth of August, the feast of the
Assumption of the Virgin Mary, after hearing Mass,
we departed from Blanc Sablon, and happily reached
mid-ocean between New Land and Brittany; and
for three days had most wretched weather and an
east wind, which, with God's help, we endured.
After this we had good weather, so that on the fifth
September of the same year we arrived at St. Malo
whence we had sailed.

## Language of the Land Newly Discovered Called New France.

This is as given in Ramusio, following the *Prima Relatione*.

| | | | |
|---|---|---|---|
| God | .......... | A feather | yeo |
| The sun | isnez | The moon | casmogau |
| The stars | furve | The land | conda |
| The sky | camet | The wind | canut |
| Day | .......... | The rain | onnoscon |
| Night | aigla | Bread | cacacomy |
| Water | ame | A man | undo |
| Sand | estogaz | The hair | hochosco |
| Sail | aganie | The eyes | ygata |
| The head | aganoze | The mouth | heche |
| The throat | conguedo | The ears | hontasco |
| The nose | hehonguesto | The arms | agescu |
| The teeth | hesangue | A woman | enrasesco |
| The nails | agestascu | Sick | alondeche |
| The feet | ochedasco | The shoes | atta |
| The legs | anondasco | Red cloth | cahoneta |
| Dead | amocdaza | A knife | agoheda |
| The skin | aionasca | Mackerel | agedoneta |
| Vergognose | ouscozon uondico | Walnuts | caheya |
| He | yea | Apples | honesta |
| Hatchet | asogne | Beans | fahe |
| Mullet | gadogoursere | A sword | achesco |
| .......... | anougaza | A branch | cacta |
| Figs | asconda | Green trees | haveda |
| Gold | henyosco | The sea | amet |
| The forehead | ansce | A ship | casaomy |

[Compare these with those given at the end of the second voyage.]

The account which Cartier gave of his First Voyage was so well received that it was certain that another would be soon made.

During the interval which elapsed between the conclusion of the First Voyage and the setting out of the second expedition, Cartier was evidently of some use to the community of St. Malo. In the Archives of St. Malo, B.B., 4-83, mention is made of a meeting, on the 22nd February, of bourgeois, and

amongst other names given is that of Cartier. This
meeting was called to consider a "collision" between
the employés of the procureur and the "gentils
hommes" of the "garrison." Cartier was also present
at another held on the 27th February, regarding an
epidemic. In the Archives of St. Malo, Delibera-
tions 1534-1535, it appears that on Wednesday, third
day of March, 1535, a meeting was held, whereat it
was stated that Cartier had stopped vessels, saying
he had the right to choose sailors to go with him to
the New Land. Some gave their consent, and it
would appear that Cartier chose the galleon of
Etienne Richomme. These are the only records of
his name at this period (Longrais' "Jacques Cartier,"
p. 24). The following is the account of the Second
Voyage.

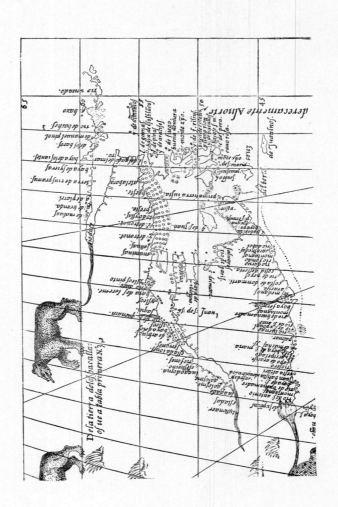

# SECOND VOYAGE.

In Ramusio, edition 1556.   Vol. iii., page 441.

In Lescarbot, edition 1612.   Lib. iii., chap. vii., *et sequitur.*
This is interpolated with extracts from Champlain.

Also in a reprint of an edition published in Paris in 1545, in
8vo., 48 pages, of which only one copy is known in Europe.

Three manuscripts in the Bibliothèque Impériale at Paris, compared with the "Brief Recit" of 1545, in the reprint mentioned
above, which is a copy of the only "rédaction française originale."

On Sunday, the sixteenth of May, 1535, the feast
of the Pentecost, Whit, (?) Easter Sunday, by order
of the captain and willingly, all went to confession
and took Holy Communion in the Cathedral of St.
Malo, after which we were all blessed by the bishop.
The Wednesday following, the nineteenth, the wind
being favorable, we set sail with our three ships, the
Grand Hermine, of 106 tons, having on board the
Captain - General (Cartier), and for chief officer
Thomas Frosmond, also Claude de Pond-Briand, son
of the seigneur of Montreuil, and cup-bearer to the
Dauphin, Charles de la Pommeraye, and others.
The second vessel, the Petite Hermine, of 60 tons,
had for captain Mace Jalobert, and for chief officer
William le Marié.   The third vessel, the Emerillon,
of 40 tons, was in charge of Captain William the
Breton, and had for chief officer Jacques Maingart.

We had favorable weather till the twentieth, when such contrary winds and tempestuous gales arose that on the twenty-fifth of June we lost each other (became separated, and did not know anything of each other till we reached Newfoundland (*terre neuve*). All of us had experienced very heavy weather since our separation. We reached land on the seventh of July, landing at Bird Island, which is fourteen leagues from the mainland; this abounds with birds, so much so, that all the ships of France could load up with them without any apparent diminution. Here we secured two boat loads full for food. This island is in latitude 40° 40′. We set sail on the eighth of July and reached the harbor of Blanc Sablon, near Castle Bay, on the fifteenth—the place we desired—and here we waited for our comrades till the twenty-sixth, on which day both vessels arrived together. We laid in a supply of water, wood and other necessaries, and set sail on the twenty-ninth at daybreak and coasted along the north coast, east-northeast, till eight o'clock in the evening, and, lowering sails, arrived between the islands situated further out than the others; we named them St. Guillaume Islands; they are about twenty leagues beyond Port Brest. The whole coast we had passed was rocky and precipitous, without soil, wood or valleys. The next day we sailed west to visit (explore) other islands, distant twelve leagues and a half. Between these islands is a bay looking north full of islands and apparently having several good harbors; we named them St. Martha Islands. Beyond which, about a league and a half, there is a very dangerous reef, with four or five points (*têtes*) above water; these lie across the bay in the route east

and west from the islands St. Guillaume and other
islands west-southwest of the St. Martha Islands,
about seven leagues. These we reached at one
o'clock, and we sailed till midnight, about fifteen
leagues, across a cape at the end of some low-lying
islands, which we named Islands St. Germain. To
the southwest of this cape, about three leagues, there
is another dangerous reef; and likewise between
Cape St. Germain and the St. Martha Islands there
is a reef, about two leagues distant, over which there
are only four fathoms, and on account of the dangerous nature of the coast we lowered sails for the
night. Next day, the last of July, we ranged along
the coast, which lies east and west, a quarter southwest, full of islands and dangerous reefs, for a distance of seventeen and a half leagues from Cap St.
Germain. After the islands are passed, there is a
fine fertile district, full of large and high trees. This
coast is sandy, without any harbors, up to Cape
Tiennot, which is situated about seven leagues to
the northwest of the islands spoken of. This cape
we recognized from our former voyage. We sailed
all night west-northwest till morning, when, the
wind changing, we anchored in a good little harbor
about seven leagues and a half from Cape Tiennot,
which harbor is between four islands jutting out
into the sea. We named the harbor St. Nicholas,
and on the nearest island we erected (*plantâmes*) a
wooden cross as a mark. It is necessary (in sailing)
to have the cross to the northeast; then turn to it
and have it to the right. The depth of water is six
fathoms, four fathoms inside; it is necessary to look
out for two reefs which are on each side, about
half a league outside. All this coast is very dan-

gerous, full of reefs; though seeming to possess several good harbors, there are only reefs and shallows. We remained in St. Nicholas harbor until Sunday, seventh of August, on which day we set sail for the land towards Cape Rapast, distant twenty leagues north-northwest. Next day the wind was contrary, and as we found no anchoring place on this south coast, we sailed to the north about ten leagues, where we reached a large and beautiful bay, full of islands and good channels and protection from any wind that can blow, and as a landmark of this bay there is a large island, like a promontory (*cap de terre*), further out than the others; and in the land two leagues off there is a mountain shaped like a stack of wheat; we named it the Bay of St. Lawrence. On the twelfth of August we left here and sailed west and reached a cape to the south, lying west a quarter south west from the Bay of St. Lawrence about twenty-five leagues. And by the two savages we had taken on our first voyage we were told that this was part of the land to the south, and that it was an island, and that to the south of it was the way or road to go to Honguedo, where we had seized them in our voyage, the year previous, to Canada. They also told us that two days' journey from the said cape and island commenced the country and kingdom of Saguenay, on the land to the north leading to Canada. Beyond the cape, about three leagues, there are a hundred fathoms and more of water; and we never saw so many whales as we did this day in the vicinity of the cape spoken of. Next day, the fifteenth of August (we passed through the straits the night before), we saw land to the south, having very high mountains. We named the above island Assumption Island. From the cape of this island to a cape of the high lands to the south, lying east-northeast and west-south-west, the distance is twenty-five leagues. And we perceived the land to the north to be higher than that on the south, for more than thirty leagues. We sailed along the south coast till Tuesday noon, when we had a west wind; we put the cape to the north to explore (visit) the high lands, and arriving there we found a low coast close to the ocean, the high mountains running east and west, a quarter west. And from our two savages we learned that this was the beginning of the Saguenay district, and that it was habitable. Here they obtained copper (*cuivre rouge*), which they call *caignet daze*. The distance between the northern and southern banks is about thirty leagues; there are more than two hundred fathoms of water. Our savages informed us that this was the river and commencement of the grand "Sileune de Hochelaga" and river of Canada; which river grows narrower going towards Canada, where it was fresh, and came from so far off that no one had ever reached its source that our savages had ever heard tell of; and, of course, only boats could be used as a means of passage. In consequence of their saying this, and as they declared there was no other channel, our captain did not wish to go further until we had visited the remaining portions of the coast and land to the north, which he had omitted to visit, as we had left the Bay of St. Lawrence to go to the south in search of another channel.

*How our Captain brought our ships about, in order to gain a knowledge of the Bay of St. Lawrence, so as to know whether there was a channel towards the north.*

Wednesday, the eighteenth of August, our captain brought the ships about, having the cape on the other side. We followed the coast lying northeast and southwest, making a half arc—very high land, unlike that to the south. Thursday following we came to several very high islands, naming them Round Islands (*Isles Rondes*), distant about forty leagues from the southern coast and three or four leagues from the northern, beyond which there is a level district full of beautiful trees, along which district we sailed on Friday. Near this are several dangerous sandbanks, uncovered at high water, and just beyond this district, ten leagues in extent, there is a river of fresh water (this is the Chischedec, most probably), which runs into the sea (so strongly) so that the water is as fresh as spring water for a league distant. We went into our boats to this river and found only a fathom and a half of water. There are in this river several kinds of fish shaped like a horse, which go to the land during the night and stay in the water during the day—so we were told by our two savages,—and we saw a large number of these fish. Next day, the twenty-first, at daybreak, we set sail and followed the northern coast to explore it further, and also the Island of Assumption (Anticosti); and when we had become certain there was no channel, we returned to our ships, which were at the seven islands spoken of before, where there is a good harbor, sandy bottom, and twenty fathoms of water. We were obliged to remain here till the twenty-fourth, on account of

storms and contrary winds, when we went to a
harbor on the southern banks eighty leagues distant.
There are three flat islands here in midstream, and
northwards, between these islands and the harbor,
there is a very large river between high and low
lands, which river has made dangerous sandbars
three leagues out; very dangerous, with two fathoms
and less of water, and these bars lie from the coast
north-northeast and south by west. The harbor
on the south coast spoken of is of little value. We
named the islands St. John Islands, as we stopped
there on that day. Before reaching this harbor
there is an island to the east about five leagues,
with no channel between it and the main land,
except for small boats. This harbor of the St
John Islands is dry at every low tide; the best place
to anchor is to the south at a small island, and on
the other side of it. We set sail from this harbor
on the first of September to go towards Canada, and
about fifteen leagues west by west there are three
islands in mid-stream, beyond which there is a very
deep and swift river, that of the kingdom and land
of Saguenay, as we were told by our savages. And
this river is between high mountains of bare rock
with but little soil, in spite of which there is a large
number of trees of various kinds which grow seem-
ingly as well on the bare rock as on fertile soil.
We saw trees large enough to make masts for a ship
of thirty tons, growing as green as possible, without
any sign of earth. At the mouth of this river we
met four canoes of savages coming towards us with
trepidation and fear; one retreated, but another
came within hearing distance of one of our savages,
who made himself known, so that they all came to

us without further fear. Next day, the second of
September, we left this river to continue our journey
to Canada, finding the eddies very swift and dangerous, because to the south of the river there are
two islands, around which for about three leagues
there are but two fathoms of water, filled with
rocks as large as casks and hogsheads. We very
nearly lost our galleon, only saving it by means of
our boats. After passing the Saguenay and these
islands, about five leagues southwest, there is another island to the north, very high; beyond this
we tried to anchor and found no bottom with one
hundred and twenty fathoms of line, a short distance from shore, so were obliged to try this side of
the island, where we anchored in thirty-five
fathoms and a good bottom. Next morning we set
sail and passed out and found a species of fish,
never before heard of or seen by us; these fish are
as large as a cod, and have a good body and head
like a greyhound; are as white as snow, without
any mark, and there are a large number in this
river; they live in salt and fresh water; the savages
call them "adhothuys." We were told that they
were excellent eating, and that they were found
only in this river. The sixth September, with good
winds, we made fifteen leagues up the river and
came to an island near the south bank, forming a
small bay, on and about which there is an immense
number of turtles and also adhothuys. There is a
swift tide here, as at Bordeaux. The island is about
three leagues long and two wide, good soil, numerous
fine trees, walnut trees (hazel nuts) filled with nuts
as large and better tasting than ones in France, but
a little harder; therefore, we named the island Isle

aux Coudres.  The seventh September, after hearing
Mass, we proceeded on our way up the river and
came to fourteen islands, seven or eight leagues
from Isle aux Coudres; this is the beginning of
Canada.  One of these islands is ten leagues long
and five wide, on which live people who catch all
kinds of fish, according to the season.  Anchoring
between this island and the north bank, we went
ashore, taking with us the two savages we had
secured the preceding voyage.  We found there
several savages (*gens du pays*), who took to flight and
would not come near us until our two began to talk
to them, telling them they were Taignoagny and
Domagaya.  As soon as they were satisfied of this,
they showed their joy, dancing and performing
antics, and came to speak to us at the boats, bringing eels and other fish, with two or three loads of
large grain (corn), which is the bread on which
they live, and several large melons (*sic*, pumpkins
probably.)  The same day several canoes of savages,
male and female, came to our ships to see and welcome our two savages, all of whom were well
received by our captain, who feasted them as well
as he could, and gave them some trifling presents,
which pleased them greatly.  Next day the seigneur of
Canada, his name being Donnacona and his title
Agouhanna, came with twelve canoes, and, leaving
ten behind as he came near the ships, approached
us with only two, accompanied by sixteen men, and
made a speech according to the fashion, contorting
the body and limbs in a remarkable way—a ceremony of joy and welcome.  This was done near the
smallest of our ships, and when he came to the
Grande Hermine, where were our Captain-General,

4

Taignoagny and his comrade, he spoke to them and
they to him, telling him what they had seen in
France and the good treatment they had received.
He was deeply pleased and asked our captain to
open his arms for an embrace—their method of welcoming. Then our captain went into the canoe of
Donnacona and ordered bread and wine for him
and his savages, which were brought, and they
were much gratified. No other presents were given.
Then they separated and Donnacona returned. Our
captain borrowed some of their canoes to go further
in search of a safe harbor for the ships, and we left
with the inflowing tide. We made about ten
leagues, following the coast line of this island, and
came to a very fine and pleasant bay. There is a
little river here and a safe harbor with three
fathoms. We named this St. Croix, on account of
the day we arrived. Around this place there is a
people (tribe) whose chief is Donnacona, and his
domicile or place of living (*demeurance*), Stadacona
is here. Fertile soil and very fruitful, numerous
fine trees, as in France ; oak, elm, ash, walnut,
yews, cedars, vines, and hawthorns, which produce
fruit as large as a damson, and other trees. There
also grows as fine hemp as in France, without any
sowing or cultivation. After visiting, and being
much pleased with this place, our captain and the
rest returned to the canoes, to go back on board
ship. And as we came out of the river we met one
of the chiefs of Stadacona, accompanied by several
men, women and children ; which chief made a
speech, according to their manner and custom, of
joy and welcome, and the women (squaws) danced
and sang without ceasing, standing in the water up

to their knees. Our captain, seeing their good disposition and intention, gave them knives and small
glass paternosters; so that even after we had left
them a league or so distant, we could perceive them
singing, dancing and showing joy at our coming.

*How our captain went back on board ship and then went to see
the island, its size and nature, and then brought the ships
to River St. Croix.*

After we had arrived with our canoes at the ships
and returned from the River St. Croix, the captain
gave orders to borrow the canoes to go and land on
the island to see the beautiful trees and the nature
of the island, which was done, and we found it full
of beautiful trees, the same as ours (in France).
And we also found a very large number of vines,
such as we had never before seen; therefore, we
called it the Isle of Bacchus. It is twelve leagues
long, covered with trees, no cultivated land; but
there are some small dwellings (wigwams) belonging to those engaged in fishing, as we have already
spoken of. Next day we set out with our ships to
take them to the St. Croix river, where we arrived
the fourteenth of the month. And there came to us
Donnacona, Taignoagny and Domagaya, with
twenty-five canoes filled with savages coming from
the place we had just left and were going to Stadacona, their home (*demeurance*), and they all came to
our ships with signs of joy, except our two savages,
Taignoagny and Domagaya, who were changed in
some manner and had no courage; would not come
on board our ships, though entreated to do so several
times; for which reason we distrusted them. The
captain asked them if they were willing to go to

Hochelaga with him, as they had agreed; they answered yes, and that they were determined to go; then all withdrew. Next day, the fifteenth, our captain went ashore to place buoys to ensure the safety of our ships, to which place came several savages, amongst others Donnacona, our two savages, and their band, but these all kept apart from us on a point on the border of a stream, none of them approaching us, while those not of their band came to us. When the captain was informed that they were there, he ordered a number of his own men to accompany him and went over to the point to Donnacona, Taignoagny, Domagaya, and the others. The captain went amongst them and Taignoagny came forward and said Donnacona was grieved for the reason that the captain and his men carried so many weapons of war, while they for their part carried none. To which the captain replied that it was the custom in France, and that *he* (Taignoagny) knew it well, and in spite of these words, Donnacona and our captain were very friendly together. We therefore perceived that what Taignoagny said originated with him and his comrade. Before separating, our captain and Donnacona gave mutual assurances of strong friendship, and all of Donnacona's people gave three shouts in a loud voice—horrible to hear—and we took our leave and went on board for that day and the next one. The sixteenth we placed our two largest ships within the bay and river, where there is at full tide three fathoms of water, and at low tide half a fathom, and we kept the other boat (galleon), the Emerillon, to take us to Hochelaga. And immediately (as soon as) that our ships were in the harbor and anchored, Donnacona, Taignoagny, and Domagaya, and more than five hundred men, women and children came, and Donnacona, with ten or twelve of the chiefs, came on board and were feasted by the captain and were given some trifling presents. Taignoagny said Donnacona was grieved because he (T.) was going to Hochelaga, and that he (D.) said the river was of no value (*i.e.*, dangerous), to which our captain made reply that he was going if it were at all possible, because he had the orders of his master, the King, to go as far as he could ; but if Taignoagny was willing to go as he had promised, a present would be given him, with which he would be highly pleased, and that they would only go to Hochelaga and then return. To which Taignoagny made answer he would not go at all. Then they withdrew to their wigwams (*maisons*). The next day, the seventeenth, Donnacona and others came, bringing eels and other fish in quantities, of which there are a large number caught in this river, as will be told hereafter. When they had come opposite our ships, they performed their customary dancing and singing. When this was finished, Donnacona put all his men on one side and made a circle in the sand, placing therein our captain and his men, and commenced a speech, holding a young girl, ten or twelve years old, by one of his hands. Then he came and gave her to our captain, immediately on which all the savages gave three cries and yells as a token of joy and alliance. The chief then presented two small boys still younger, one after the other, and the same ceremonies and cries ensued. Our captain thanked the chief for these presents. Then Taignoagny told the captain that the girl was the daughter of the chief's sister and one of the boys was the brother of him who spoke (Taignoagny). And these were given with the hope that we would not go to Hochelaga. To which our captain made reply that if they were given with the hope that he would not go to Hochelaga, they would have to take them back, and that he would not take anything to deter him from going, as he had his orders to do so. On which words, Domagaya, companion of Taignoagny, told the captain the presents had been made through affection and as a pledge of friendship, and that he was pleased to go to Hochelaga with him, for which reason Domagaya and Taignoagny had bitter words together. Therefrom we saw that the latter was unreliable (worthless), that he was traitorous and malicious, as we had previously thought, on account of evil actions we had seen him do. Our captain placed the young savages on board ship and caused to be brought two swords, a large wide brass basin and a wash basin, and gave them to Donnacona, who was much pleased and thanked our captain, and he gave orders to all his people to dance and sing and entreated our captain to have a cannon discharged, of which Taignoagny and Domagaya had told him, and which he had never seen or heard. The captain consented and gave orders to fire a dozen with their shot through the woods beyond the savages. At which they were so astonished, they thought the heavens had fallen upon them, and took to howling so terribly that it seemed to be the case that hell was empty. Before they withdrew, Taignoagny sent word that those on the Emerillon, which was out in the channel, had killed two of their men by the shot; on hearing which all retired in great haste, as if we had wished to kill them also.

The story was not true, as no shot had been fired from the Emerillon.

*How Donnacona, Taignoagny and others devised a cunning plan and disguised three men as devils, pretending to come from their deity Cudragny, to prevent us from going to Hochelaga*

Next day, the eighteenth, in order to prevent us going to Hochelaga, they thought out a grand scheme as follows:—They dressed up three men as devils with horns as long as the arm, and they were covered with the skins of black and white dogs. Their faces were painted black as coal, and they were placed in a concealed canoe. The band came to us as usual, the others waiting in the woods without appearing for about two hours for the time and tide for the arrival of the above canoe; at which time they all came out of the forest and showed themselves before our ships without approaching any nearer. According to their plan, Taignoagny saluted our captain, who asked if he wanted our boat; the former replied not for the present, but that by-and-by he would come on board, and immediately the canoe, with the three disguised as devils with long horns on their head arrived, and the one in the centre made a strange speech as they approached. They passed along by our ships in their canoe without turning their eyes upon us, and continued till they struck hard upon the shore with their canoe; then immediately Donnacona and his people took the canoe and the three men who lay in the canoe as if dead and carried all into the woods, about a stone's throw distant, and not a single savage was left in front of our ships. From within the woods they began a talking and a preaching which we could hear on the ships, and this went on for about half an hour; after which Taignoagny and Domagaya came forth, walking towards us, hands joined, their hats under their arms, and attracting much attention; and Taignoagny began to talk, uttering three times "*Jesus, Jesus, Jesus,*" and lifting his eyes towards heaven, and then Domagaya began to say "*Jesus Maria.*" Jacques Cartier looked towards heaven also. He, noting their behavior and actions, asked them what was the matter and what was new. They replied they had sad news, saying, "Nenny is it good" (*i.e.*, it is not good). The captain repeated his question and they replied that their god called Cudragny had spoken at Hochelaga, and that the three men (devils) had come from him with the information that there was so much snow and ice there that all would die. On hearing these words we all laughed and told them that their god Cudragny was but a fool, did not know what he said,—to tell his messengers so, and that Jesus would preserve them from cold if they would believe in Him. Then Taignoagny asked the captain if he had spoken to Jesus, who answered that the priests had, and that we should have fine weather. They thanked the captain and returned into the forest to inform the others, who immediately came out of the woods, pretending to be pleased with the words of the captain. To prove it, they came at once before the ships and together gave three cries or yells—their sign of joy, danced and sang; but in contradiction Taignoagny and Domagaya told our captain that Donnacona was unwilling that any of them should go with the captain to Hochelaga. The captain told them that if they had not determined to go with him with good heart, they could remain behind, and that he would not be prevented from going.

*How our captain and all the nobles (gentils hommes), with fifty sailors, departed from Canada with the galleon (Emerillon) and the two boats, to go to Hochelaga, and what was done by them on the river.*

Next day, the nineteenth of September, we set sail with the galleon and two boats to go up the river with the tide, finding on both banks as fine lands as one could hope to see. Springs of water and beautiful trees, and so many vines loaded with grapes along the river that it appeared as if they had been planted by man rather than otherwise, but they are neither cultivated nor pruned; the grapes are neither so large nor sweet as ours. We found numerous huts (*maisons*) on the banks, in which live those who fish, and these savages came to us in as great friendliness as if we belonged to the country, bringing us numbers of fish; and for what we gave them extending their hands to heaven and making manifestations of joy. We reached a place about twenty-five leagues from Canada, called Ochelay, which is a strait with a strong and dangerous current and full of rocks.

Amongst others came a grand chief, who made a great speech in coming alongside, telling us by signs with his hands and other ceremonies that the river was very dangerous a little in advance of us, and warning us to take care. He presented to our captain two of his children, of whom the captain took the little girl, seven or eight years old, and refusing to take the boy, aged two or three years, as

he was too small. Our captain feasted the chief and
his band as well as he could and gave some little
presents, after which they went on shore. The
chief and his wife came afterwards to see his little
girl and brought gifts to our captain. From the
nineteenth to the twenty-eighth we had been
sailing up the river without losing an hour, during
which time we saw as fine a country and soil as
could be wished for, full of fine trees, such as
oak, elm, walnut, cedar, spruce, ash, osiers, birch,
willows, and plenty of vines, which vines were so
loaded with grapes that our sailors came on board
with as many as they could carry. There are large
numbers of cranes, swans, outards, geese, plover,
pheasants, partridges (grouse), blackbirds, thrushes,
doves, goldfinches, canaries (*sic*), nightingales, solitary sparrows and other birds, as in France, and
very numerous. The twenty-eighth September we
arrived at a large lake five or six leagues wide and
twelve long; and we sailed all day without finding
any where more than two fathoms of water, with no
tide, and we came to the end of the lake, where
there appeared to us to be no passage or outlet. It
appeared to be shut in without any river, and we
found only a fathom and a half of water; so we
concluded to anchor outside and look for a channel
with our boats. We found four or five rivers all
running into the lake and flowing from Hochelaga.
There are bars in these channels made by the current, over which there is but one fathom of water.
After passing these bars there are four or five
fathoms—this at the dryest time of the year—as we
saw by the waves of these waters that they are
more than three fathoms deep. These rivers sur-

*These Rivers*

surround five or six pretty islands, forming the end (upper) of this lake. About fifteen leagues further up they form one river. This day we were on one of these islands and met five savages who were trapping wild animals, and they came to our boats as familiarly as if they had seen us all their lives, showing no fear; and our boats coming to shore, one of the savages took our captain in his arms and carried him ashore as easily as if he werë a child of five years, so large and strong was this man. We found a large number of wild rats, which live in the water and are good to eat. They gave some to our captain, who gave them knives and beads in return. We asked them by means of signs if this was the way to Hochelaga. They replied yes, and that we had still three days' journey.

*How the captain fitted up the boats, in order to go to Hochelaga, and left the Emerillon on account of the difficulty of the passage ; how we reached Hochelaga and the reception given us on our arrival.*

Next day, the twenty-ninth of September (old style), our captain seeing it was impossible to proceed with the Emerillon, provisioned and fitted up the boats, taking provisions for as long a time as possible, and as much as the boats would hold, set out on the voyage, accompanied by the following nobles (*gentils hommes*) :—Claude du Pont Briand, cup bearer of the Dauphin ; Charles de la Pommeraye, Jehan Gouion, Jehan Poullet, with twenty-eight sailors, amongst whom were Mace Jallobert and Guillaume le Breton, who had charge of the two other ships under the captain, to go up the river as far as we could ; and we voyaged with good

weather till the second of October, when we arrived
at Hochelaga, distant from the place where we had
left our galleon (Emerillon) forty-five leagues.
While on the journey we were given fish by the
savages, also other edibles; they showed much joy
at our coming. To attract them to us and hold
their friendship our captain gave them knives,
beads and other trifles, pleasing them greatly. On
our arrival at Hochelaga more than a thousand
savages gathered before us, men, women and children; they received us as well as a parent does a
child, showing great joy. The men danced in a
group together, the women in another, and the children in another, and after this they brought us a
great number of fish and much of their bread, made
with large grain (corn), which they threw into our
boats in such quantities that it seemed to be falling
from the air. Our captain, seeing this, went ashore
with several others. As soon as he had landed, they
all gathered round him and the others, welcoming
them warmly; and they brought their children in
their arms to touch the captain and others, making
an occasion of joy which lasted more than half an
hour. Our captain, seeing their good-will, caused
the women to sit down in rows and gave them tin
bells and such trifles, and to some of the men he
gave knives. Then he returned to the boats to sup
and pass the night. All night the savages remained
on the shore near our boats making fires, dancing
and crying out "Aguyaze," which is their word of
welcome and joy.

*How the captain and the others, with twenty well armed sailors,*
*went to the town of Hochelaga ; the situation of the village.*

Next day, early, the captain put on his regimentals
and put his men in proper order to go and see the
town and dwelling place of this (people) tribe, and
the mountain adjacent to the town. With the
captain went the (*gentils hommes*) nobles and twenty
sailors ; he left the rest to guard the boats, and took
three men of the said town of Hochelaga to lead
the way to it. We found the road a well beaten
one and as fine a soil as one could wish to see, filled
with oaks as fine as in the forests of France, the
ground underneath which trees was covered with
acorns. Having walked about a league and a half,
we met one of the chiefs of the town, accompanied
by several savages, which chief made us stop at a
fire he had made on the road, which we did, and
then he made a long speech, as is their custom of
showing joy and friendship, and greeted our captain
and his associates warmly. The captain gave him
a couple of axes, knives and a crucifix, which he
made him kiss and hang it round his neck ; for
which the captain was thanked. We marched
further, and about half a league further from there,
we began to see ploughed land and large fields of
their wheat, which is like the grain of Brazil, as
large or larger than a pea. on which they live, as we
do, on wheat, and amidst these fields is situated the
town of Hochelaga, near to and touching a mountain, which is around it, very fertile and cultivated,
from the summit of which one can see far off. We
alled this mountain " le Mont Royal." The town
is round in shape and enclosed with three rows of

timbers (stakes) in the shape of a pyramid, crossed on top, having the middle stakes perpendicular, and the others at an angle on each side, well joined and fastened (*consu*) in their fashion. It is of the height of two lances and there is only one entrance to the town through a gate (door) which can be barred. At several points within the enclosure there are stages (platforms) and ladders to get up on them, which stages are provided with rocks and stones as a means of defence. There were in the town about fifty huts or houses, each fifty steps or more in length and twelve or fifteen wide, all made of wood covered with bark and strips of wood as large as a table, sewn well together artificially in their way; within there were several rooms. In the centre of the town there was a large space used as a fireplace, where they eat in common, each man retiring afterwards to his rooms with his wife and children. Likewise they have lofts or granaries in their houses, where they store their corn, out of which they make their bread, which they call "Carraconny." The following is their method of making it : They have mortars of wood similar to those used for making hemp, and they pound the corn into flour (*en pouldre*), then gather it into dough, make it into cakes, which they place upon a large hot rock, then cover it with hot stones; and thus they bake their bread instead of an oven. They make also much soup with this corn and beans and peas, of which they have a plenty; also large cucumbers and other fruits. They have large vessels in their houses, like casks, in which they place their fish, which they smoke during the summer and eat during the winter; and of these they

lay in big stores, as we know by experience. All
their food is eaten without a taste of salt. They
sleep on bark, spread on the ground with wretched
skins of animals, of which they also make their
clothes, such as squirrels, beavers, martens, foxes,
lynxes, deer and others; but the greater part of the
savages go almost naked. The most precious article
to them is " Esurgny," which is white as snow, and
which they secure in the river in the following
manner:—When a man has merited death, or when
they have taken any of their enemies prisoners, they
kill them and make incisions in the thighs, shoulders, etc.; let the body down to the bottom of the
river, leave it there ten or twelve hours, bring it
up and find in the incisions the said shellfish
(*cornibotz*), out of which they make beads, and make
use of these as we do of silver or gold, and consider
them the most precious of all things in the world.
These will stop bleeding at the nose, as we proved
in our own experience. All this tribe live by
ploughing and fishing alone, as they do not esteem
the goods of this world, having no knowledge of
them, and never leave their country, and are not
nomadic (*ambulataires*) like those of Canada and the
Saguenay, notwithstanding which the Canadians
are subject to them, as are eight or nine other tribes
living on the banks of this river.

*How we arrived at the town and the reception accorded
us ; how the captain gave presents, and other matters
which will be seen in this chapter.*

After we had arrived near the town a large number
of the savages came about us and greeted us warmly

according to their fashion. We were conducted by
our guides to the centre of the town, where there is
an open space about a stone's throw square, and
here they made us signs to come to a halt, and suddenly gathered the girls and women, of whom a
certain number had infants in their arms, and they
came and rubbed our faces, arms and other portions
of our bodies that they could touch, crying with
joy to see us, greeting us as warmly as they knew
how, and making signs to us it would please them
if we would touch their infants. After this, the
men made the women withdraw and sat down on
the ground around us, as if to enter into some mystery (*jouer un mystère*). Suddenly several women
returned, each of whom brought a square mat similar
to tapestry; they spread them out and made us sit
down on them. This being done, their king and
chief, whom they call Agouhanna in their tongue,
was carried in by nine or ten men. He was seated
on a large deer skin, and they placed him on the
mats near our captain, making signs to us he was
their king and chief. Agouhanna was about fifty
years of age, no better dressed than the others,
except that he had a red crown on his head, made
out of the skin of a hedgehog. All his limbs were
disabled. Having saluted our captain welcoming
us, he showed his arms and limbs to the captain,
making signs that he would be pleased to have him
touch them, and the captain rubbed them with his
hands; and immediately were brought to the
captain several sick people—blind, lame, those with
only one eye, cripples, and some with their eyelids
hanging down on their cheeks; setting and laying
themselves down near our captain, so that he might

touch them ; as if they thought God had sent him
to cure them. Our captain, seeing their simplicity
and faith, read the Gospel of St. John, namely the *In
principio* ("In the beginning, etc."), and, making the
sign of the cross over the sick, prayed to God to
give them knowledge of our holy faith, and grace
to receive Christianity and Baptism. Then the
captain, for a couple of hours, read to them the
Passion of our Saviour ; and, although they could
not understand, they paid great attention, looking
up to heaven and making motions as they saw us
do ; after which the captain put all the men on one
side, the women on another, and the children on
another, and gave to the leaders hatchets, knives to
others, beads to the women, and then he threw
among the young people small rings and tin images
of the *Agnus Dei*, with which they were much
pleased. Then the captain ordered the trumpets
and other musical instruments to be sounded, at
which they were astounded. Then, taking our
leave, we went out, and the women came before us
bringing us fish, soup, beans and other things to
feast us ; but as their food was not to our taste,
having no flavor (salt), we thanked them, making
signs to them that we were not hungry. After we
were outside the town, several men and women
came to lead us up the mountain, which we had
named Mont Royal, distant about a quarter of a
league. Having reached the summit, we could see
more than thirty leagues round about. Towards
the north, a range of mountains, lying east and west,
and also one to the south. Between these ranges
the soil is fertile, level, and easy of cultivation, and
in the middle of the plain we could see the river

5

further than the place where our boats were ; also a
rapid as impetuous as possible, impossible of ascent
by us, though we saw it was large and deep beyond
this, going towards the southwest, and passing
three beautiful round mountains, which we could
see, and estimated to be distant about fifteen leagues
from us. Those who had guided us made signs
that there were three rapids in the river, but we
could not make out how far distant, as we could
not speak to them. We made out, however, that
after passing these rapids here near us, one could
navigate for more than three months up the river ;
and beyond they showed us a large river flowing
near the mountains to the north, which comes from
the west like our river (St. Lawrence). We thought
it to be the river that passed by the country of the
Saguenay. Without our asking any question or
making any sign, one of the savages took the chain
of the captain's silver whistle and the case for a
dagger, made of metal yellow like gold, which he
hung on the side of one of our sailors, and told us
they could get that up that river, and that there
were Agouiandas there, meaning ferocious people,
armed to their finger-ends, showing us the shape of
their arms (*armures*), which are made out of cord and
wood, tied and woven together, and we were given
to understand that these Agouiandas carried on war
continually, tribe against tribe, but we could not
make out how far it was to their country. Our
captain showed them some copper (*cuivre rouge*),
which they call " caignet dazé," and pointing
towards the country spoken of, asked them by signs
if any came from there, and they shook their heads,
meaning no ; and they made signs that it came from

SKIP THIS ~~PAGE~~ PAGE (OUT OF ORDER)

Saguenay. Having seen and heard these things we returned to our boats, attended by a large number of these people, and part of them, seeing our men were weary, made horses of themselves and carried us. Reaching our boats, we went to our galleon (Emerillon) to make sure it was all right. Our departure caused these people great regret; they followed us as long as they could along the river. We reached our Emerillon on Monday, the fourth day of October. On Tuesday we set sail to return to the Province of Canada, to the River St. Croix (St. Charles), where our ships were. On the seventh we came to the mouth of a river which comes from the north, running into the river (St. Lawrence), at the mouth of which are four small islands full of trees. We called this river the River of Faith; and as one of the islands juts out in advance of the others, and can be seen from a distance, the captain erected a large cross on the point. He gave orders to get the boats ready to go up this river with the tide, to know its character (nature), which was done, and we rowed all day up the river, and as we discovered nothing, we returned and resumed our journey.

*How we arrived at the St. Croix; the condition in which we found our ships; how the chief of the country came to see our captain; how our captain went to see him; and a custom of this tribe.*

Monday, the eleventh October, we arrived at the river St Croix, where were our ships, and found our mates and sailors who had remained behind. They had made a fort in front of the ships out of large pieces of timber placed perpendicularly side by side, guns at all points, and were in a good condition of

defence against the power of the whole country.
As soon as the chief was told of our arrival, he came
the next day, the twelfth, with Taignoagny, Domagaya and others; a grand *fête* was given to our
captain, and all were joyous at our return. The
captain received them well, though they had not
deserved it. Donnacona entreated the captain to go
next day and visit Canada, which he promised to
do. Next day, the thirteenth, the captain, with the
nobles and fifty sailors in proper order, went to see
Donnacona and his people, distant from our ships a
league. They call their village (*demeurance*) "Stadacona." On reaching it, the people came from their
houses about a stone's throw, and there gathered
together, sat down in their usual way and fashion,
the men on one side and the women on the other,
dancing and singing continually. Our welcome and
greetings over, the captain gave the men knives
and other articles of little value, and causing the
women and girls to pass before him, he gave each
one a ring of tin. They thanked the captain, who
was then led by Donnacona and Taignoagny, to
see their houses, all filled with provisions for the
winter, and Donnacona showed us the scalps of five
men's heads, spread out on a board, like the skin of
an animal. Donnacona told us these had been taken
off the "Tondamaus" to the south, at war with them
continually. He told us that two years previously
these Tondamaus came even to the river to attack
them, at an island opposite Saguenay, where they
(Donnacona's men) were passing the night waiting
to go to Honguedo to make war, with about two
hundred men, women and children. They were
surprised during the night in the fort they had built,

which the Tondamaus set on fire on all sides, and as
they came out all except five were killed, who
escaped, and they were very bitter over this severe
loss, averring that they would be revenged. We
then returned to our ships.

*How the people of this country live ; their condition, belief
and customs.*

This people have no belief in God, for the reason
they believe in one they call "Cudragny," and they
say he often speaks to them and tells them what to
do. They say also that when he is provoked he
throws dirt in their eyes. They also believe that
when they die they go to the stars and go down
below the horizon like them, and they go away to
pretty fields full of fine trees, flowers and delicious
fruits. After they had told us all, we showed them
their error and told them Cudragny was a bad spirit
who misuses them. We told them there was only
one God, who lived in Heaven, who gives us all we
need, and is creator of all, and in Him only ought
we to believe, and that it was absolutely necessary
to be baptized or else go to hell, and we told them
other points of our belief. These they easily accepted,
and called their Cudragny, Agouianda (malicious).
They several times entreated the captain to baptize
them, and Donnacona, Taignoagny, Domagaya, and
all the tribe came, but not knowing their wish and
that they had only taken the faith for a time, the
captain made excuses to them. He told Taignoagny
and Domagaya that he would explain it to them, and
that he would return in another voyage and would
bring with us priests and chrism (holy oil), giving

as an excuse that baptism could not be effected without the chrism, which they believed, as several young people had witnessed the ceremony in Brittany; and they were very joyous at our promise to return. This people (tribe) live in community of goods (*communauté de biens*) like the Brazilians; cover themselves but scantily with the skins of wild animals. In winter they wear stockings and shoes (moccasins) made of skins, and in summer they go barefoot. They believe in the order of marriage, but have two or three wives; if the husband dies, none of the wives remarry, and remain in mourning all their lives. They paint their faces with charcoal and grease to the thickness of the back of a knive blade, and are thereby known as widows. They have one vicious custom regarding their young women, who, as soon as they reach a certain age, are put into a house free to all men who wish to go, until they make a choice of a husband. And these affairs we saw ourselves; we saw the houses as full of young women as the boys' schools in France are of boys. And furthermore, these houses are used for gambling purposes, where they hazard all, even the skins covering their persons. They do not work hard; plough their land with little sticks, half as large as a little sword, where they sow their corn, which they call "Osizy." This is as large as a pea, and the same as grows in Brazil. They have likewise great quantities of large melons (pumpkins), cucumbers and gourds, peas and beans of all colors, unlike ours (in France). They have a grass (plant) of which they gather a large quantity for the winter's use, which is held in great favor and used by the men only and in the following manner :—They dry it in the sun

70

and carry it in a little pouch of skin around their
necks, with a horn (cornet) of stone or wood (a pipe);
they make this grass into powder and put it into one
of the ends of the horn, then place a hot coal on the
top of it and suck at the other end, filling their
bodies with smoke so that it comes out from their
mouths and nostrils like from the pipe of a chimney ;
they say this keeps them healthy and warm, and
they never go anywhere without having these
articles. We tried this smoking, putting some of the
smoke in our mouths, which was as hot as pepper.
The women work far more than the men at the fishing, which is important, as well as other labors.
And all—men, women and children—endure cold
better even than the wild animals ; for in the greatest
cold we experienced, which was very severe, the
majority of them came naked over the snow and ice
daily to the ships, which we would hardly have
believed if we had not seen it. They catch, during
the time of snow and ice, numbers of moose (?),
deer, bears, hares, martens, foxes and others. They
eat their meat raw, after drying it in smoke, and in
the same way their fish. With what we had seen
and could make out of this tribe, it seems to me it
would be easy to tame (civilize) them. May God in
His mercy bring this about. Amen.

*How the savages brought fish and other food daily to our
ships; and how, influenced by Taignoagny and Domagaya, they ceased coming and held no talk with us.*

From day to day the people came to our ships,
bringing large quantities of eels and other fish in
exchange for our goods, such as knives, beads and
other trifles which pleased them very much; but we

perceived that Taignoagny and Domagaya were evil disposed and gave them to understand that our goods were of no value, and that they ought to receive hatchets instead, notwithstanding that the captain gave them numerous presents which they kept asking for. The captain was warned by a chief of the village of Hogauchenda to beware of Donnacona, Taignoagny and Domagaya, as they were traitors. Others of Canada also warned us, and we also saw that, out of malice, they wished to obtain from us the three children that Donnacona had given the captain, and they managed to keep many of the people away from the ships. In consequence of this the captain was on his guard; and through the influence of Taignoagny and Domagaya, the savages kept away from us four or five days, except a few who came, however, in great fear and trembling.

*How the captain, fearing treachery, strengthened the fort; how they held a talking, and the return to us of the girl who had fled.*

Seeing their unfriendliness and fearing treachery, and that they might come in a large body against us, the captain had the fort strengthened with large and deep ditches, with a drawbridge and more timbers. Orders were given to have the night-watch in the future consist of fifty men for the four watches, and at each watch trumpets were blown; and Donnacona, Taignoagny and Domagaya, noticing the strengthening of the fort and the good watch kept, were grieved to be in the bad graces of the captain, and sent men several times, pretending they were elsewhere, to see if we would show displeasure; but we paid no attention whatever and gave no sign. Donnacona, Taignoagny and Domagaya came several times to speak to the captain, the river being between them, asking the captain if he was angry, and why he did not go to Canada to see them. The captain told them they were traitors and malicious, as he had been informed, and as he had perceived in several ways, such as their not keeping their promise to go to Hochelaga, and also their taking away the girl they had given him, and other falseness which he spoke of ; but, in spite of all, if they wished to act right and forget their unfriendliness, he woutd forgive them and they could come on board and be welcomed as before. For these words they thanked the captain and promised to bring back the girl who had fled, within three days. The fourth of November Domagaya and six others came to the ships to tell the captain that Donnacona had gone into the country in search of the girl, and that he would bring her the following day. He said, further, Taignoagny was very sick and asked the captain to send him a little salt and bread, which the captain did, and sent word to Taignoagny that it was Jesus who was angry with him on account of the evil tricks he wished to play us. Next day, Donnacona, Taignoagny, Domagaya and others came, bringing the girl, giving her back to the captain, who paid no attention, and said he did not want her, and for them to take her back again. To which they replied, making the excuse that they had not told her to run away, but that she had done so because she had been beaten, and they renewed their request to the captain to take her, and brought her themselves to the ship, after which the captain ordered bread and wine to be brought and treated them ; they then took their leave, after which we continued to exchange visits in as friendly a manner as previously.

*Of the depth and length of the river, the animals, birds, fish and other things we saw, and the position of the places.*

The river (St. Lawrence) begins after Assumption Island, Honguedo and the Seven Islands are passed. The distance across is between thirty-five and forty leagues, with over two hundred fathoms in depth in places. The safest navigation is on the southern side ; to the north, about seven leagues distant from the Seven Islands, are two large rivers which come from the mountains of Saguenay and make several very dangerous bars in the river. At the mouths of these rivers we saw several whales and sea-horses. Beyond these islands there is a small river which forms marshes for three or four leagues, in which are an extraordinary number of birds. From the mouth of the river to Hochelaga it is more than three hundred leagues. The commencement is at that river that comes from Saguenay, which latter comes out from between high mountains on the north and enters before the district of Canada is reached, and is very deep, straight, and of dangerous navigation. After passing this river, the district of Canada is reached, where there are several peoples (tribes) in villages not stockaded. There are several small and large islands, amongst them one more than ten leagues long, full of beautiful high trees and many vines. There is a channel on both sides, the better one being on the south side. On the west side is a fine, safe harbor for ships, where there is also a narrow and deep strait with a strong current. But it is only a third of a league in length, beyond which there is high land, all cultivated—as fine soil as can be seen anywhere, and this is the village and home of Donnacona and of the two savages we had taken on our first voyage. It is called Stadacona, and before coming to this place there are the homes (*demeurance*) of four tribes, namely, Araste, Starnatau, Tailla, which is on a mountain, and Satadiu, then Stadacona, under which high place to the north is the river and bay of St. Croix, where we stayed from the fifteenth of September up to the sixth of May, 1536. Our ships had been left here, as has been mentioned. Beyond this is the village and tribe of Tequenondabi, which is on a mountain, and Hochelay, which latter is a level country. The land on both banks of the river up to Hochelaga and beyond is as fertile and level as can be seen anywhere. There are some mountains a distance from the river (St. L.), from which mountains flow several rivers into the (main) river. All this country is well covered with trees of various kinds and vines, except around the villages which have been cleared to build their houses and for cultivation. There are large numbers of deer, bears and other animals. We saw the tracks of an animal with only two feet, which tracks we followed a long distance over sand and mud, its feet are larger than the palm of the hand; hares, martens, foxes, squirrels, very large rats (musk), beavers, wolves, rabbits, and others. The savages cover themselves with skins, having no other garb. There are cranes, swans, outardes, white and grey wild geese, plovers, ducks, blackbirds, thrushes, doves, goldfinches, canaries (linnets or finches), linnets, nightingales, solitary sparrows and other birds, as in France. As has been mentioned in previous chapters, fish of all the kinds ever heard of abound in the river; for, from its mouth up to its end (*i.e.*, as far as they went), in proper season will be found nearly all kinds of salt and fresh water fish; also will be found in Canada large numbers of whales, cod, sea-horses, and adhothuys, a kind of fish we had never seen or heard of. They are as large as a cod, white as snow, have a body and head like a greyhound, and stay in brackish water between the river of Saguenay and Canada. There will also be found in June, July and August plenty of mackerel, mullet, barr (*sartres*), large eels and other fish, also as good as in the river Seine, and plenty of lampreys and salmon. In Canada are bass, trout, carp, bream, and other fresh water fish. And all the fish are taken in large numbers in their season by the tribes for food.

*Information given us by the savages after our return from Hochelaga.*

Since our return from Hochelaga with the Emerillon and the two boats, we held friendly intercourse with the tribe nearest our ship, except that we had some difficulties with a few ill-disposed savages, concerning which the others were grieved and provoked, and we were told by Donnacona and others that the river spoken of before was called the Saguenay river, and goes (comes from) as far as Saguenay, which is to the west-northwest. After eight or nine days' journey only boats can be used in it; but the proper way to the Saguenay is by the river as far as Hochelaga, then by a river which comes from the Saguenay. Between the said rivers, a month's travel distant, is a tribe, attired in cloth as we are, and there are numerous tribes and villages, good people, possessing large quantities of gold and copper; and all the land between Hochelaga and Saguenay is an island, surrounded by rivers. And further on this river enters two other large lakes; then is found a fresh-water sea, of which no one had seen the end, at least amongst those who had been told of it by the people of Saguenay. They told us they had never been there; also that at the place where we had left our galleon (Emerillon) when at Hochelaga, there is a river which goes to (comes from) the south-west, and a month's journey up it leads to a country where there is no ice or snow, but that the inhabitants are constantly at war. And in this country there are oranges, almonds, walnuts, apples, and other kinds of fruit in great abundance. They informed us that the peoples there dressed in skins as they themselves did. In answer to one question, whether there was any gold or copper there, they answered no. I think this country to be towards Florida, judging from their description.

*Of a severe sickness which visited the people of Stadacona and with which from our going amongst them we were also attacked and so severely that twenty-five of our people died.*

In December we became aware that death was visiting the tribe of Stadacona to so great a degree that already more than fifty had passed away, for which reason we forbade them coming to our fort or amongst us. In spite of this we were sorely visited with the epidemic, unknown and mysterious to us;

the sick lost flesh and their legs became swollen, muscles contracted and black as coal; covered with purple blood blisters. Then the disease affected the hips, thighs and shoulders, arms and neck. In each instance, the mouth was so diseased that the flesh fell off, even to the roots of the teeth, and nearly all the teeth fell out. And so much did the sickness prevail amongst us that, in February, out of one hundred and ten souls that we had been, not ten were free from it; and one could not assist another. Our condition was pitiable, considering the place where we were; for the savages came every day in front of our fort, though but few of us saw them. We had eight dead, and fifty others were so sick we had given up all hope of them. Our captain, seeing how prevalent the sickness and suffering were, made all pray, and caused an image of the Virgin Mary to be placed against a tree at a distance of an arrow's flight from our fort across the snow and ice, and he gave orders to say Mass there the following Sunday, and all those who could go, the well and the sick, went in a procession singing the seven psalms of David, the litany, praying the Virgin Mary that her child Jesus should have pity on us. Having said Mass, our captain made a vow to make a pilgrimage to Notre Dame des Roquemadon, if God should permit him to return to France. This day Phillipe Rougemont, a native of Amboise, died (passed away) at the age of twenty-two years; and because we knew nothing of the disease, the captain caused the body to be opened, to see if we could gain any knowledge how to save the rest, if possible. It was seen that the heart was white and shrivelled, surrounded with considerable brown water, the liver

healthy, but the lung was black and mortified, and
all the blood gone from above the heart; for when
the body was opened, a large quantity of black diseased blood came out from above the heart. Likewise the spleen near the chine had a cut about the
size of two fingers' breadth, as if done with a stone.
One of the thighs was cut, which was very black on
the outside, but the flesh was of good color underneath. He was then buried as best we could. God
in his grace, have mercy on his soul and forgive
all his sins. Amen. And the sickness continued
from day to day to such a degree that soon on
all the three ships there were not three well men, and
on one of the ships there was not a man well enough
to go below deck to get water either for himself
or the others. Several more died, and on account of
our lack of physical strength, we buried them merely
under the snow, as the ground was frozen so hard
we could not dig it in our weak state, and we were
in great fear lest the savages should perceive our
distress and defenceless condition, and to conceal it
from them when they came near our fort, our captain, whom God had preserved, worked before their
eyes with two or three men, sick and well, who followed him. When they were outside the fort, he pretended to be desirous of beating them, shouting and
throwing sticks at them, sending them on board ship
and making signs to the savages that he had need of
his men on board the ships, some to caulk, some to
make bread and do other work, and that it was not
good for them to be idle on shore. This they believed, and the captain had noises made on board the
ships with sticks and stones, as if caulking were
being done. At this time we were so cast down by

the sickness that we should have lost all hope of
ever returning to France, if God, in his infinite
mercy and goodness, had not had pity on us and
given us knowledge of a remedy for all sickness, the
best ever found on this earth, as will be related in
another chapter.

*The length of time we were in the snow and ice at St. Croix, and
the number of persons that died from the time the sickness
began up to the middle of March.*

From the middle of November till the fifteenth of
April we were continuously shut in by the ice,
which was more than two fathoms thick. On the
ground there was more than four feet of snow, being
higher than the sides of our ships, for the same
period of time. Our drinkables were frozen in their
casks; the ice was four inches thick on the hull and
rigging, and all the river, being fresh water up to
Hochelaga, was also frozen. During this time we
lost by death twenty-five souls, all good men, and
now there were not more than fifty whom we considered strong and vigorous; the remainder all sick,
with the exception of three or four who were free
altogether. But God, in His holy mercy, had pity
on us and gave us knowledge of a remedy and cure
as detailed in the following chapter.

*How by the grace of God we had knowledge of a tree by which
we were cured after using it; the method of using it.*

One day the captain, seeing the sickness so
prevalent, and his men so overcome by it, being
outside the fort and walking on the ice, saw a
band (group) of the people of Stadacona approaching, in which was Domagaya, whom the captain

had seen very ill with the disease ten or twelve days previously. He had then one of his knees swollen to the size of a child of two years; all his muscles contracted; his teeth had fallen out, and his jaws had been mortified and diseased. Our captain seeing Domagaya healthy and well, was overjoyed, hoping to learn from him how he was cured, so as to cure his own men. When they had come near the fort, the captain asked him how he had been cured. Domagaya replied he had taken the juice and grounds of the leaves of a tree, which had cured him, and this was the peculiar remedy for the malady. The captain asked if there was any of the remedy thereabouts, as he wished to cure his servant (valet), who had caught the disease in Canada, while they were with Donnacona—not wishing to let him know how many of his men were sick. Then Domagaya sent two women to get some; they brought nine or ten branches and showed us how to take off the bark and leaves and to put all to boil in water, then to drink of it for two days and put the grounds on the swollen limbs. They told us this tree cured all sickness; they call the tree in their language "ameda." At once our captain made a drink of it to give those who were sick, though there were none anxious to try it except one or two, who took the risk. As soon as they had done so the effect was miraculous, for the reason that all the sickness with which they were affected left them after drinking two or three times, and they became well; so much so that some who had had venereal disease for five or six years previous to this sickness were cured completely. Having perceived this, there was so much haste to get the remedy that it looked

6

as if they would kill one another in order to be the first to get it ; so that a tree, as large as an oak in France, was consumed in six days, which produced an effect that had all the doctors of Lourain and Montpellyer been present, with all the drugs of Alexandria, they could not have affected as much in a year as this tree did in six days, for it was so beneficial that all those who were willing to use it were cured and recovered their health, thanks be to God.

*How Chief Donnacona, Taignoagny and others went deer hunting ; did not return for two months ; and on their return they brought with them a large number of people we were not accustomed to see.*

While sickness and death reigned in our ships, Donnacona, Taignoagny and others went to hunt deer and stags (*daims*), which they call in their language aiounesta and asquenondo, for the ice had disappeared from the river channel so they could navigate it. Domagaya and others told us they would be absent about fifteen days, which we believed, but they did not return for two months, which made us suspect that they had gone to get together a large number of people to give us trouble, as they had perceived our weakened state ; although we had put affairs in such good shape that, if all the people of the country had been there, they could have done nothing more than look at us. While they were away, large numbers came daily to our ships as usual, bringing the fresh meat of deer and stags, and fresh fish of all kinds, which they sold us at a high price, or else preferred to take it away, as they needed them themselves, the winter had been so long.

*How Donnacona returns to Stadacona with a large number*
*of people ; plays sick to avoid coming to see the captain,*
*thinking the captain would go to him.*

The twenty-first day of April Domagaya came to
us with several savages, fine looking and strong,
whom we had not been accustomed to see. He said
Donnacona would come the next day and bring deer
meat and other venison. The next day, the twenty-
second, Donnacona arrived. He had brought to
Stadacona a large number of people ; we knew not
for what reason or purpose ; but there is a proverb,
"He who is watchful, loses nothing," which we
were, of necessity, as we were so weakened by sickness and the loss of men that we were (on our departure) obliged to leave one of our ships at St. Croix.
The captain was apprised of his coming and that he
had brought such a number of people. Domagaya
came and told the captain of it, without wishing to
cross the river between us and Stadacona as usually
done, which led us to believe there was some
treachery afoot. Seeing which, the captain sent his
body servant, Charles Guyot, who was more so than
any other liked by the savages, to see what was
going on, and he was to go and see Donnacona, with
whom he had lived a considerable length of time,
and he took a trifling present for him. As soon as
Donnacona knew of his coming he pretended to be
ill and went to bed, telling the servant he was sick.
He went to see Taignoagny, and found the houses
everywhere so full of savages that one could hardly
move, which was strange and unusual ; and Taignoagny did not wish the servant to go in other
houses, and returned half way with him and told
him that if the captain wished to take a chief named

Agouhanna, who had vexed him, with him to France, the chief would be given up to him. It would be done if the captain wished it, and the servant could return next day with his answer. When the captain was informed of the number of people at this place, for a purpose unknown to him, he determined to play them a trick and seize Taignoagny, Domagaya and other important ones. He was determined also to take the Chief Donnacona back to France to relate to the King the wonders of the world he had seen in the western countries. He had assured us he had been in the Saguenay kingdom, where are infinite gold, rubies and other riches; and there are white men there as in France, and dressed in woollen clothing. And he had seen another country where the people do not eat or digest, etc. He also had been, so he said, in the country of the Picquemyans, and other countries where the inhabitants have only one leg, and other curious matters long to relate. This chief, Donnacona, is an old man, and had travelled, as long as he could remember, through countries, across rivers, streams and by land. After the servant had delivered his message and told what Taignoagny had said, the captain sent him back the next day to tell Taignoagny to come and see him, express his wishes, and that he would be well received and welcomed. Taignoagny sent word he would come the next day, and that he would bring Donnacona and the other chief (Agouhanna) who had displeased him. This did not happen, and two days passed without their coming. During this time no one from Stadacona came to the ships, as they were accustomed to do, but fled from us as if we had wished to kill them. Thus we became aware of their ill-will, and because they perceived that the people of Sicadin came about us, to whom we had abandoned the bottom of the ship we left behind us, for them to procure the old nails. The third day following, they of Stadacona came from the other side of the river; the majority of them crossed without difficulty in their canoes, except Donnacona, who was unwilling to do so, and Taignoagny and Domagaya talked together for more than an hour before they agreed to cross. Finally they came to speak to the captain, and Taignoagny entreated the captain to take the chief (Agouhanna) to France. He refused, saying the King had forbidden him to bring man or woman to France, but he could take back two or three children to learn the language; however, he would take the chief to Newfoundland and leave him on an island. The captain said this to reassure them and to secure Donnacona, who had remained on the water. These words pleased Taignoagny greatly, who was very anxious never to go back to France. He promised to come the next day, that of the Holy Cross, with Donnacona and the other savages of Stadacona.

*How, on the day of the Holy Cross, the Captain erected a cross in our fort; how Chief Donnacona, Taignoagny, Domagaya and the tribe came; the capture of the chief.*

The third of May, the fête of the Holy Cross, as a solemn tribute, the captain had a cross erected, about thirty-five feet high, under the cross bar of which there was a shield (escutcheon) of wood, of the arms of France, and on it was written in Attic letters: FRANCISCUS PRIMUS DEI GRATIA FRANCORUM REGNAT. About noon came men, women and children of

Stadacona telling us that Donnacona, Taignoagny, Domagaya and others were coming, which gave us much satisfaction, as we hoped to seize them. They came about two o'clock; and when they had come down to the ships, our captain went to greet Donnacona, who warmly received him, but kept his eye on the forest and was in great fear. Then came Taignoagny, who told Donnacona not to enter the fort. One of the savages brought fire from the fort, and a fire was lit by the chief. The captain invited him to come and eat on board ship, as customary. He likewise asked Taignoagny, who said he would go by and by. They entered the fort. Previous to this the captain was informed by Domagaya that Taignoagny had spoken badly (suspiciously), and had told the chief not to go on board the ships. Our captain seeing this, went outside the enclosure and saw the women departing by advice (warning) from Taignoagny, so that a large number of men only remained. Then the captain ordered his men to seize Taignoagny, Domagaya, and two other leaders he pointed out, after the others went away. Soon the chief came into the fort with the captain, but immediately Taignoagny came in to bring him out. Our captain seeing there was no other way, gave the order to seize them, when his men came out and seized the chief and the others, as had been designed. The Canadians (savages) seeing the capture, began to run and flee like sheep before the wolf, some across the river, others into the forest, each one looking out for his own safety. The capture effected, and the others having fled, the captives were put in a secure place.

*How the Canadians (savages) came during the night down to
the ships, seeking their people, during which night they
yelled and howled like wolves ; the discussion and demand
made next day ; their presents to our captain.*

As soon as it was night, they came down to the
ships in large numbers, howling all night ceaselessly
like wolves, "Agouhanna! Agouhanna!" thinking
to speak to him ; but the captain would not have it
for the time being, nor till up to noon next day, for
which reason they thought we had killed and
hanged them. About noon they returned in about
as large a number as we had seen of them together
at one time during the voyage ; keeping themselves
hid in the woods, except some who cried out at the
top of their voices for Donnacona. Then our captain
gave orders to put the chief in an elevated position
that he might speak to his people. The captain told
him he would be well treated, and that after he had
related to the King of France what he had seen in
the Saguenay and other places, he could return in
ten or twelve months, and that the King would
make him a grand present ; all which pleased Donnacona greatly, and he told his people, who gave
three wonderful cries, in token of joy. Donnacona
and his people made speeches to each other, which
we could not understand, as we did not know the
language. Our captain told Donnacona to have some
of his people come on board, as they could talk better
together, and that they would be safe. Donnacona
did so, and a boat load of them came on board.
They renewed their talks, praising our captain, and
presented him with twenty-four strings or necklaces
(*colliers*) of esurgny, which is their most precious
possession, valuing it more than gold or silver.

Having talked enough, and seeing there was no escape for their chief, and that he was obliged to go to France, he ordered them to bring him food for his voyage. Our captain presented Donnacona with two brass fry pans or buckets, hatchets, knives, beads and other trifles which pleased him. He sent them to his wives and children. The captain also gave presents to those who had come to talk with Donnacona, for which they were grateful. They then left and went back to their homes (*logis*).

*How next day, the fifth of May, the people returned to speak to their chief, and how four women came on board with provisions.*

On the fifth of May, very early in the morning, the savages came in very large numbers to speak to their chief and sent a boat, which they call in their language, "Casnouy," in which were four women ; no men, for fear we would keep them. They brought a large quantity of provisions ; namely, corn, meat, fish and other kinds of their food. These women, having reached the ships, the captain told them to tell the other women that he would return within twelve moons (months), and would bring Donnacona back to Canada. This he said to content them ; they were greatly pleased, and made signs that if he would do this they would make him many presents. Then each of them gave the captain a *collier* of esurgny, and then went to the other side of the river, where were the people of Stadacona, and departed, taking leave of their chief.

Saturday, the seventh, we set sail from the harbour of St. Croix and anchored below the Island of Orleans, about twelve leagues from St. Croix, and on

Sunday we reached Isle aux Coudres, where we remained till Monday, the sixteenth, waiting for the river to become calmer, as it was too rough and dangerous for us to descend the river, and waiting for good winds ; during which period several canoes of people subject to Donnacona came from the river of Saguenay, and when Domagaya told of their capture and how Donnacona was being taken to France, they were much astonished.  They came alongside to speak to him, and he told them he would return in twelve moons ; that he was treated well by the captain and the rest, for which they all with one voice thanked the captain, and gave Donnacona three packages of beaver and seal skins, also a large knife of copper, which is found in Saguenay, and other articles.  They gave the captain also a *collier* of esurgny, in return for which the captain gave them ten or twelve hatchets, with which they were over- joyed, and thanked the captain.  The channel on the north side of this island is safer than the southern, which is full of rocks, reefs and bars.  The sixteenth of May we set sail from Isle aux Coudres and anchored near an island fifteen leagues further down ; this island is about five leagues in length.  We stayed here all night, hoping to pass through the dangers of Saguenay the next day, which are great. In the evening we saw a large number of hares, and named the island Hare Island.  During the night the wind became so violent and unfavorable that we thought it expedient to return to the Isle aux Coudres, which we had left, because there was no other channel between the islands ; and we were here till the twenty-first, when we had a good wind and went as far as Honguedo, which channel had not been discovered before.  And we ran across the Cape di

Prato (Cape Farillon), which is the commencement of the Bay of Chaleurs; and as the wind was favorable, we carried sail day and night. And next day we came to the Island of Brion, which we wished to do to shorten our voyage. These two lands lie southeast and northwest, a quarter east and west; the distance between them is fifty leagues. The Island of Brion is in latitude 47½°. Thursday, the twenty-sixth, fête of the Ascension of our Saviour, we came to a country of low sandy ridges, eight leagues southwest of the Isle of Brion, above which are large lands full of trees, and there is an enclosed sea, into which we could not discover any channel or entry. Friday, the twenty-seventh, on account of the wind blowing on shore, we returned to the Isle of Brion, where we stayed till the 1st of June, and visited a high land to the southwest, apparently an island, along which we coasted twenty-two leagues and a-half, during which we discovered three islands near the sandy ridges, which are islands, and the said high and level land (above them) is the mainland and points northwest; after which we returned to the cape of the said land, which cape has three peaks (points) of great height. There is a great depth of water, and such a swift tide that it could not be more so. We arrived this day at Cape Lorraine, which is in latitude 46½°, to the south of which cape is a low lying land, apparently the mouth of a river, but possessing no good harbour; beyond which, to the south, we saw another cape, which we named Cape St. Paul, in latitude 47¼°. On Sunday, the fourth of June, the fête of the Pentecost, we came to the coast east-southeast of Newfoundland, about twenty-two leagues distant from Cape St. Paul. As the wind was unfavorable, we stopped at a harbour, which we named the Bay of the Holy Ghost, until Tuesday, when we coasted along to the St. Pierre Islands. During this journey we saw several islands and very dangerous reefs lying in the route, east-southeast and west and north-west, two, three and four leagues out in the sea. While we were at the St. Pierre Islands, we met with several ships from France and Brittany. We remained here from the eleventh of June, the fête of St. Barnabé, till the sixteenth, when we set sail, reached Cape Race, and entered a harbour named Rougnouse, where we took in water and wood for our voyage, and left there one of our boats. From here we set sail on the nineteenth. With the favoring winds we had, we reached, on the 6th day of July, 1536, the harbour of St. Malo, by the grace of God, whom we beseech, having finished our voyage, to grant us His mercy and paradise to come. Amen.

LANGUAGE OF THE DISTRICTS AND KINGDOMS OF HOCHELAGA AND CANADA, OTHERWISE NAMED BY US NEW FRANCE.

1. Segada.
2. Tigneny.
3. Hasche.        (Asche).
4. Hounacon.      (Hannaion).
5. Ouiscon.
6. Indahir.
7. Ayaga          (Aiaga).
8. Addegue        (Addigue).
9. Madellon.
10. Assem.

(These Indian words are as given in the reprint and in Ramusio, also those which follow.)

The names given to the various parts of the human body :—

| | | |
|---|---|---|
| The head, | Aggourzy, | (Aggonzy). |
| The forehead, | Hetguenyascon, | (Hergenmascon). |
| The eyes, | Hegata, | (higata). |
| The ears, | Ahontascon, | (abontascon). |
| The mouth, | Escahe, | (esahe). |
| The teeth, | Esgongay, | (esgongai). |
| The tongue, | Osuache, | (osnache). |
| The throat, | Agouhon, | (agouhon). |
| The chin, | Hebehin, | (hebelim). |
| The face, | Hogouascon, | (hegouascon). |
| The hair, | Aganiscon, | |
| The arms, | Aiayascon, | (aaiayascon). |
| The armpits, | Hetnanda, | |
| The ribs, | Aissonne, | |
| The stomach, | Aggruscon, | |
| The belly, | Escheheuda, | |
| The thighs, | Hetnegradascon, | |
| The knees, | Agochinegodascon, | |
| The legs, | Agouguenehonde, | |
| The feet, | Ohchidascon, | |
| The hands, | Aignoascon, | |
| The fingers, | Agenoga, | |
| The nails, | Agedascon, | |
| The genital organ (man) | Aynoascon, | |
| " " " (woman), | Castaigne, | |
| A man, | Aguehan, | (Aguehum). |
| A woman, | Agrueste, | (Agrueste). |
| A boy, | Addegasta, | |
| A girl, | Agnyaquesta, | |
| An infant, | Exiasta, | |
| A dress, | Cabata, | |
| A waistcoat, | Coioza, | (caioza). |
| Socks, | Henondoua | (hemondoha). |
| Shoes, | Atha, | |
| Shirts, | Anigona, | (amgona). |
| A hat, | Castnea, | |
| Corn, | Osizy, | |
| Bread, | Carraconny, | |
| Water, | Ame, | |
| Flesh, | Quaheriascon, | |

| | | |
|---|---|---|
| Fish, | Queion, | |
| Plums, | Honnesta, | |
| Figs, | Absconda, | |
| Grapes, | Ozaha, | (ozoba). |
| Nuts, | Quaheya, | (quahoya). |
| A hen, | Sahomgahoa, | |
| Lamprey, | Zysto, | |
| A salmon, | Ondaccon, | |
| A whale, | Ainnehonne, | |
| An eel, | Esgneny, | |
| A squirrel, | Caisgnem, | |
| A snake, | Undeguezi, | |
| Turtles, | Heuleuxime, | |
| Wood, | Conda, | |
| Leaves, | Hoga, | |
| Their deity, | Cudragny, | (cudonagny). |
| Give me a drink, | Quazahoa quea, | |
| Give me a lunch, | Quazahoa quascahoa, | |
| Give me supper, | Quazahoa quatfream, | |
| Let us go to bed, | Casigno agnydahoa, | |
| Good day, | Aignaz, | |
| Let us play, | Casigno candy, | |
| Come and speak to me, | Asigni quaddadia, | |
| Look at me, | Quagathoma, | |
| Be quiet, | Aista, | |
| Let us go to the boat, | Casigno casnouy, | |
| Give me a knife, | Quazahoa agoheda, | |
| A hatchet, | Addogne, | |
| A bow, | Ahena, | |
| An arrow, | Quahetam, | |
| Let us go and hunt, | Quasigno donassent, (donascat) | |
| A deer, | Aionnesta, | |
| Stags (moose ?) | Asquenondo, | |
| A hare, | Sourhamda, | |
| A dog, | Agayo, | |
| Geese, | Sadequenda, | |
| The road, | adde, | |
| Cucumber seed, | } casconda, | |
| Melon seed, | | |
| To-morrow, | Achide, | |
| The sky, | quenhia, | |
| The earth, | damga, | |
| The sun, | ismay | (isnay). |

| | | |
|---|---|---|
| The moon, | assomaha, | |
| The stars, | signehoham, | |
| The wind, | cahoha, | |
| The sea, | agogasy, | |
| The waves of the sea, | coda, | |
| An island, | cohena, cahem, | |
| A mountain, | ogacha. | |
| Ice, | honnesca, | |
| Snow, | canisa, | camsa. |
| Cold, | athan, | |
| Warm, | odazan, | (odazani)(odayan) |
| Fire, | azista, | |
| Smoke, | quea, | |
| House, | canocha, (canoca) | (quanocha). |
| Beans, | Sahe, | |
| Town (village), | canada, | |
| My father, | addathy, | |
| My mother, | adanahoe, | |
| My brother, | (addagnin) | (addagrim). |
| My sister, | adhoasseue, | |

Those of Canada say that in a country a month's journey distant from Hochelaga, can be had cinnamon and cloves. They call cinnamon, adhotathny; cloves, canonotha.

In the manuscripts of this Second Voyage are given additional words, the principal ones being :—

| | |
|---|---|
| That is worthless, | sahanty quahonquey, |
| Adieu (good-by), | hedgaguehanygo, |
| Sing, | theguehoaca, |
| Laugh, | cahezem, |
| Cry, | agguenda, |
| Dance, | thegoaca, |
| Freshwater, | ame, |
| My friend, | agnaise, |
| Run, | thedoathady, |
| The smoke hurts my eyes, | quea quanoague eguta, |
| Some one is dead, | Camedane, |
| The title of Donnacona as Chief is | Agouhanna, |
| Bad, wicked, | agojuda, |
| Ugly, | aggousay, |
| What they smoke, | quiecta, |

| | |
|---|---|
| Grass, | hanneda, |
| Rats, large as rabbits and smelling of musk, | houtthe, |
| Too old to walk, | agoudesta, |
| My cousin, | hegay, |
| My nephew, | ynadiu, |
| My wife, | ysaa, |
| My child, | aguo, |
| Walk, | quedaque, |
| Where do you come from ? | Canada undagneny, |
| Give it to some one, | taquenonde, |
| Keep it for me, | sodanadega mesganiy, |
| Where is he gone ? | quanehoesnon, |
| Shut the-door, | asnodyau, |
| Go and get water, | sagethemme, |
| Go and find somebody, | achedascone, |
| High, | estahezy, |
| Small, | estahagza, |
| Large, | houganda, |
| Hail, | hocquehin, |
| Evening, | angau, |
| Night, | aubena, |
| Day, | adeyahon, |
| When they make an exclamation, they say, | aggondec. |

As is related in the account of the Second Voyage, Cartier took back with him to France several Indians, and an effort was made to instruct them, so that they might act as interpreters. They were baptized on the 25th March, 1538. The change of climate and living proved unhealthy for them, and all died except one young girl, before any service could be had of them. A new expedition was determined upon under François de la Roque, Sieur de Roberval, whom the King, by letters of the 15th January, 1540, and 7th February, registered at Paris, the 26th, named as his lieutenant-general in the " new lands of Canada, Hochelaga and Saguenay, and thereabouts," to establish "la foi chretienne." On February 6th he took the oath in presence of Cardinal de Tournon.

On February 27th, Paul d'Angelhon, known as Sainterre, was appointed his lieutenant, and, on March 9th, Roberval was authorized to impress criminals for his expedition. Royal letters, given at St. Prix, the 17th October following, and signed by Henry the Dauphin, on the 20th, appointed Jacques Cartier " Captain-General and Master Pilot" of all the ships and vessels sent on this expedition.

[The sending out of this expedition had been delayed by troubles in France ; the Emperor Charles had invaded Provence, and the city of Marseilles was in a state of seige. He had troops also in Picardy. The Spaniards also were hostile. Francis, however, concluded a truce of ten years with the Emperor on the 18th June, 1538.]

On November 3rd, orders were given for fifty additional criminals to be impressed for the expedition, and on December 12th, it is to be noted that the King complains of delay in the starting out of the expedition. At present we have no record of anything of interest till the 19th of May, 1541, when certain criminals arrive at St. Malo for the " voyage to Canada." Amongst them was one young *fiancée* of eighteen years, guilty of no crime, who followed a brutal criminal.

And on this day Jacques Cartier made his will, which is to be found in two places, in the register of the sheriff (Greffe d'office) of St. Malo, dated 12th November, 1541, and in the Archives d'Ile-et-Vilaine, under date 17th November.

And on the day following, the 20th, Cartier appears as a witness in a suit concerning a common brawl, in which he had no active part.

There was some trouble between Roberval, who was imperious, and Cartier, the particulars of which are as yet unknown. Roberval was at St. Malo about the time of Cartier's departure, if not on the day itself, and it is probable he made loans at this time in Cartier's name, for the non-payment of which Cartier and his relatives were afterwards reproached.

Five vessels, totalling about four hundred tons, having been got ready, Cartier set out from St. Malo on the 23rd May, 1541, leaving Roberval in France; the latter was to follow him with the balance of the material for the founding of the projected colony.

On July 10th, it is recorded that the King thought it strange Roberval had not left.

On August 18th, Roberval writes from Honfleur he will leave in four days. This is according to Gosselin, and that he sailed from Honfleur on August 22nd, 1541. Other authorities state he sailed from La Rochelle.

Cartier, after a long and stormy voyage, reached Ste. Croix, the St. Charles, on the 22nd or 23rd of August, but preferred to winter his vessels four leagues further, at the mouth of a river near Cap Rouge, where he built a fort, giving it the name of Charlesbourg Royal, in honor of Charles, Duke of Orleans. He sent back to France two of his vessels, under command of Mace Jalobert, his brother-in-law, and Etienne Noel, his nephew. These left on the 2nd September with letters for the King. These were met at St. John by Roberval.

Cartier himself went up the river the 7th September, above Hochelaga, to explore the rapids and falls

7

which impede navigation, returning and wintering at the fort.

During the fall of 1541, Roberval sent Sainterre back to France, and the latter was sent back by the King on January 26th, 1542, with provisions.

In the meantime, Jalobert and Noel had arrived in France with news of the death of La Bouille, Cartier's right-hand man.

Cartier, having no news of Roberval at the end of May, 1542, set sail for France, and, it is claimed, met Roberval with three ships and two hundred men at St. John, who had arrived on the 17th June, 1542, having left France on the 16th April. This is in accordance with one account. Cartier refused to return with him and, setting sail during the night, reached St. Malo and paid off his men.

The other account of Roberval is, as stated above, he set sail from France August 22nd, 1541, and wintering somewhere, receiving provisions from the King during the summer of 1542, built France Roy. On September 9, 1542, he pardons Sainterre for mutiny, and, after wintering, is brought back by Cartier in the summer of 1543. The writer is not inclined to accept this account, believing rather that he left France on the 16th April, 1542. Still the accounts are so incomplete as yet, and there yet remain registers to be gone over, that no decided opinion can be given as yet. The following is the account of the Third Voyage :—

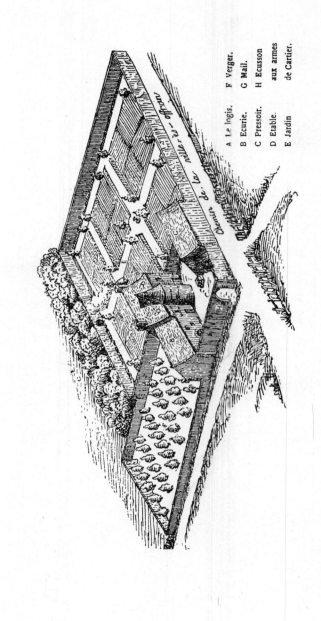

Chemin de la ville — *Offran*

A  Le logis.
B  Ecurie.
C  Pressoir.
D  Etable.
E  Jardin
F  Verger.
G  Mail.
H  Ecusson
   aux armes
   de Cartier.

# THIRD VOYAGE.

In Hakluyt, Vol. iii., page 232, ed. 1600.
In Pinkerton's Voyages. Vol. xii., 665, 1812.
Voyages de Descouvert au Canada. Quebec, 1843.
Hakluyt was reprinted in 1809. Churchill's Voyages also contain Cartier's Voyages.

*The Third Voyage of Discovery made by Captain James Cartier, 1540, unto the Countries of Canada, Hochelaga, and Saguenay.*

King Francis the First, having heard the report of Captain Cartier, his Pilot-General, in his two former voyages of discovery, as well by writing as by word of mouth, touching that which he had found and seen in the western parts discovered by him in the parts of Canada and Hochelaga, and having also seen and talked with the people, which the said Cartier had brought out of these countries, whose name Donnacona, and others; which after that they had been a long time in France and Britain (?), were baptized at their own desire and request, and died in the said country of Britain (?), and albeit His Majesty was advertised by said Cartier of the death and decease of all the people which were brought over by him (which were 10 in number), saving one little girl about ten years old, yet he resolved to send Cartier, his pilot, thither again, with John Francis de la Roche, Knight, Lord of Roberval, whom he appointed his lieutenant and governor in the countries of Canada and Hochelaga, and the said Cartier captain-general and leader of the ships, that they might discover more than was done before in the former voyages, and attain (if it were possible) unto the knowledge of the country of the Saguenay, whereof the people brought by Cartier, as is declared, made mention unto the King that there were great riches and very good countries, and the King caused a certain sum of money to be delivered to furnish out the said voyage with five ships, which thing was performed by the said Monsieur Roberval and Cartier. After that they had agreed together to rig the said five ships at St. Malo and Brittany, where the two former voyages had been prepared and set forth.

And the said Monsieur Roberval sent Cartier thither for the same purpose. And after that Cartier had caused the said five ships to be built and furnished and set in good order, Monsieur Roberval came down to St. Malo and found the ships fallen down to the road, with their yards across, full ready to depart and set sail, staying for nothing else but the coming of the General, and the payment of the furniture (equipment). And because Monsieur Roberval, the King's lieutenant, had not as yet his artillery, powder and munitions and other things necessary come down, which he had provided for the voyage in the countries of Champaigne and Normandy, and because the said things were very necessary, and that he was loth to depart without them, he determined to depart from St. Malo to Roan (Rouen) and to prepare a ship or two at Honfleur, whither he thought his things were come. And that the said Cartier should depart with the said five ships which he had furnished, and should go before.

Considering also that the said Cartier had received letters from the King, whereby he did expressly charge him to depart, and set sail immediately upon the sight and receipt thereof, on pain of incurring his displeasure, and to lay all the fault upon him. And after the conclusion of these things, and the said Roberval had taken muster and view of the gentlemen, soldiers and mariners which were retained and chosen for the performance of the said voyage, he gave unto Cartier full authority to depart and go before, and to govern all things as if he had been there in person; and himself departed from Honfleur to make his further preparation.

After these things thus despatched, the wind coming fair, the foresaid five ships set sail together, well furnished and victualled for two years, the 23rd May, 1540. And we sailed so long with contrary winds and continual torments, which fell out by reason of our late departure, that we were on the sea with our said five ships full three months before we could arrive at the haven and port of Canada, without ever having in all that time thirty hours of good wind to serve us to keep our right course; so that our five ships through those storms lost company one of another, all save two that kept together, to wit, that wherein the Captain was, and the other wherein went the Viscount of Beaupré, until at length, at the end of one month, we met altogether at the haven of Carpont in Newfoundland.

But the length of time we were in passing between Britainy and Newfoundland was the cause that we stood in great need of water, because of the cattle, as well as goats, hogs, as other beasts, which we carried for breed in the country, which we were constrained to water with cyder and other drink.

Now, therefore, because we were the space of three months sailing on the sea and staying in Newfoundland, waiting for Monsieur Roberval, and taking in of fresh water, and other things necessary, we arrived not before the haven of Sante Croix in Canada (where in the former voyage we had remained eight months) until the 23rd day of August, in which place the people of the country came to our ships, making show of joy for our arrival ; and namely he came thither which had the rule and government of the country of Canada, named Agona, which was appointed king there by Donnacona, when in the former voyage we carried him into Frauce ; and he came to the captain's ship with six or seven boats and with men, women and children.

And after the said Agona had enquired of the captain where Donnacona and the rest were, the captain answered that Donnacona was dead in France, and that his body rested in the earth, and that the rest stayed there as great lords, and were married, and would not return back unto their country. The said Agona made no show of anger at all these speeches, and I think he took it so well because he remained lord and governor of the country by the death of the said Donnacona. After which conference the said Agona took a piece of tanned leather of a yellow skin, edged about with esnogny (which is their riches, and the thing which they esteem most precious, as we esteem gold), which was upon his head instead of a crown, and he put the same upon the head of our Captain, and took from his wrists two bracelets of esnogny, and put them upon the Captain's arms, coiling him about the neck, and shewing unto him great signs of joy, which was all dissimulation, as afterwards it well appeared. The Captain took his said crown of leather and put it again upon his head, and gave him and his wives certain small presents, signifying unto him that he had brought certain new things, which afterwards he would bestow upon him for which the said Agona thanked the Captain. And after that he had made him and his company eat and drink, they departed and returned to the shore with their boats.

After which things the said Captain went, with two of his boats, up the river beyond Canada and the port of Sainte Croix, to view a haven and a small river which is about four leagues higher, which he found better and more commodious to ride in and lay his ships than the former. And, therefore, he returned and caused all his ships to be before the said river, and at a low water he caused his ordnance to be planted to place his ships in more safety, which he meant to keep and stay in the country, which were three; which he did the day following, and the rest remained in the road in the midst of the river (in which place the victuals and other furniture were discharged which they had brought) from the 26th August until the 2nd September, what time they departed to return to St. Malo, in which ships he sent back Mace Jaloberte, his brother-in-law, and Stephen Noel, his nephew, skillful and excellent pilots, with letters unto the King, and to advise him what had been done and found, and how Monsieur de Roberval was not yet come, and that he feared that by occasion of contrary winds and tempests he was driven back again into France.

The said river is small, not past fifty paces broad, and ships drawing three fathoms water may enter in at full sea; and at a low water there is nothing but a channel of a foot deep or thereabout.

On both sides of the said river there are very good and fair grounds, full of as fair and mighty trees as any be in the world, and divers sorts which are about ten fathoms higher than the rest, and there is one kind of tree above three fathoms, about which they in the country call Hauneda, which has the most excellent virtue of all the trees in the world, whereof I will make mention hereafter. Moreover, there are great store of oaks, the most excellent that ever I saw in my life, which where so laden with mast that they cracked again; besides this there are fairer arables (maples?), cedars, beeches and other trees, than grow in France; and hard unto this wood, on the south side, the ground is all covered with vines, which we found laden with grapes as black as mulberries, but they be not so kind as those of France, because the vines be not tilled, and because they grow of their own accord. Moreover, there are many white thorns, which bear leaves as big as oaken leaves and fruit like unto medlars. To be short, it is as good a country to plough and manure as a man should find and desire.

We sowed seeds here of our country, as cabbages, turnips, lettuces, and others, which grew and sprung up out of the ground in eight days.

The mouth of the river is towards the south, and it windeth northward like unto a snake; and at the mouth of it, towards the east, there is a high and steep cliff, where we made a way in manner of a pair of stairs, and aloft we made a fort to keep the nether fort and the ships, and all things that might pass as well by the great as by this small river.

Moreover, a man may behold a great extension of ground apt for tillage, straight and handsome and somewhat inclining towards the south, as easy to be brought to tillage as I would desire, and very well replenished with fair oaks and other trees of great beauty, no thicker than the forests of France.

Here we set twenty men to work, which in one day had laboured (worked) about an acre and a half of the said ground, and sowed it, part with turnips, which at the end of eight days, as I said before, sprang out of the earth; and upon that high cliff we found a fair fountain (spring), very near the said fort; adjoining whereunto we found good store of stones, which we esteemed (thought) to be diamonds.

On the other side of the said mountain and at the foot thereof, which is towards the great river, is all along a goodly mine of the best iron in the world, and it reacheth even hard unto our fort, and the land which we tread on is perfect refined mine (ore), ready to be put into the furnace; and on the water's side we found certain leaves of fine gold, as thick as a man's nail. And westward of the said river there are, as hath been said, many fair trees, and toward the water, a goodly meadow full of as fair and goodly grass as ever I saw in any meadow in France; and between the said meadow and the wood are great store of vines; and beyond the said vines the land groweth full of hemp, which groweth of itself, which is as good as may possibly be seen, and as strong. And at the end of the said meadow, within 100 paces, there is a rising ground which is of a kind of slate-stone, black and thick, wherein are veins of mineral matter, which shew like gold and silver ; and throughout all that stone, there are great grains of the said mine. And in some places we have found stones like diamonds, the most fair, polished, and excellently cut that it is possible for a man to see ; when the sun shineth upon them, they glitter as it were sparkles of fire.

The said Captain, having dispatched two ships to return to carry news according as he had in charge from the King, and that the fort was begun to be builded, for preservation of their victuals and other things, determined, with the Viscount of Beaupré and other gentlemen, masters and pilots chosen for counsel, to make a voyage with two boats furnished with men and victuals, to go as far as Hochelaga, of purpose to view and understand the fashion of the saults of water, which are to be passed to go to Saguenay, that he might be readier in the spring to pass farther, and in the winter time to make all things needful in a readiness for their business.

The aforesaid boats being made ready, the captain and Martin de Painpont, with other gentlemen and the remnant of the mariners, departed from the said place of Charlesbourg Royal the 7th September, in the year aforesaid 1540. And the Viscount de Beaupré staid behind for the guarding and governing all things in the fort.

And as they went up the river, the Captain went to see the Lord of Hochelay, which dwelleth between Canada and Hochelaga ; which, in the former voyage, had given unto the said Captain a little girl, and had oftentimes informed of the treasons which Taignoagny and Domagaia (whom the captain in his former voyage had carried into France) would have wrought against him; in regard of which his courtesy the said Captain would not pass by without visiting of him; and to let him understand that the Captain thought himself beholden unto him, he gave unto him two young boys, and left them with him to learn their language, and bestowed upon him a cloak of Paris red, which cloak was set with white and yellow buttons of tin, and small bells, and with all he gave him two basins of laton (brass), and certain hatchets and knives. Whereat the said lord seemed greatly to rejoice, and thanked the Captain. This done, the Captain and his company departed from that place.

And we sailed with so prosperous a wind, that we arrived the eleventh day of the month at the first sault of water, which is two leagues distant from the town of Tutonaguy. And after we were arrived there, we determined to go and pass as far up as possible with one of the boats, and that the other should stay there till it returned, and we double manned her to row up against the course or stream of the said sault.

And after we had passed some part of the way from our other boat, we found bad ground and great rocks, and so great a current that we could not possibly pass any farther with our boat; and the Captain resolved to go by land to see the nature and fashion of the sault.

And after that we were come on shore, we found hard by the waterside a way and beaten path, going

towards the said saults, by which we took our way.
And on the said way, and soon after, we found an
habitation of people, which made us great cheer, and
entertained us very friendly. And after that we
had signified unto them, that we we going towards
the saults, and that we desired to go to Saguenay,
four young men went along with us to show us the
way, and they brought us so far that we came to
another village or habitation of good people, which
dwell over against the second sault; which came
and brought us of their victuals, as pottage and fish,
and offered us of the same.

After that the captain had enquired of them, as
well by signs as words, how many more saults we
had to pass to go to Saguenay, and what distance
and way it was thither, this people showed us, and
gave us to understand, that we were at the second
sault, and that there was but one more to pass, that
the river was not navigable to go to Saguenay, and
that the said sault was but a third farther than we
had travelled, shewing us the same with certain
little sticks, which they had laid upon the ground
in a certain distance, and afterwards laid other small
branches between them both, representing the
saults; and by the said mark, if their saying be true,
it can be but six leagues by land to pass the said
saults.

After that we had been advertised by the said
people of the things above mentioned, both because
the day was far spent, and we had neither drank
nor eaten the same day, we concluded to return
unto our boats, and we came thither, where we found
great store of people, to the number of 400 persons
or thereabout, which seemed to give us very good

entertainment, and to rejoice of our coming; and, therefore, our Captain gave each of them certain small trifles, as combs, brooches of tin and copper, and other small toys; and unto the chief men, every one his little hatchet and hook, whereat they made certain cries and ceremonies of joy.

But a man must not trust them for all their fair ceremonies and signs of joy, for if they had thought they had been too strong for us, then they would have done their best to have killed us, as we understood afterwards.

This being done, we returned with our boats, and passed by the dwelling of the Lord of Hochelay, with whom the Captain had left the two youths as he came up the river, thinking to have found him; but he could find nobody save one of his sons, who told the Captain he was gone to Maisouna, as our boys also told us, saying, that it was two days since he departed. But in truth he was gone to Canada, to conclude with Agona what they should do against us.

And when we were arrived at our fort, we understood by our peeple that the savages of the country came not any more about our forts as they were accustomed, to bring us fish, and that they were in a wonderful doubt and fear of us. Wherefore our captain having been advertised by some of our men which had been at Stadacona to visit them, that there was a wonderful number of the country people assembled together, caused all things in our fortress to be set in good order, etc.

[The rest is wanting.]

*The voyage of John Francois de la Roche, Knight, Lord of
Roberval, to the countries of Canada, Saguenay and
Hochelaga, with three tall ships and two hundred persons,
both men, women and children, begun in April, 1542, in
which parts he remained the same summer, and all the
next winter.*

Sir John Francis de la Roche, Knight, Lord of Roberval, appointed by the King as his lieutenant-
general in the countries of Canada, Saguenay, and
Hochelaga, furnished three tall ships, chiefly at the
King's cost, and having in his fleet 200 persons, as
well men as women, accompanied with divers gentlemen of quality, as namely, with Monsieur Saine-
terre, his lieutenant, l'Espiney, his ensign, Captain
Guinecourt, Monsieur Noir Fontaine, Dieu Lamont,
Frote, la Brosse, Francis de Moire, la Salle, and
Royeze, and John Alphonse of Xanctoinge, an excellent pilot, set sail from Rochel, the 16th April
1542. The same day, about noon, we came athwart
of Chef de Boys, where we were enforced to stay the
night following. On Monday, the 17th of the said
month, we departed from Chef de Boys. The wind
served us notably for a time, but within a few days
it came quite contrary, which hindered our journey
for a long space, for we were suddenly enforced to
turn back, and to seek harbour in Belle Isle on the
coast of Bretaigne, where we stayed so long and had
such contrary weather by the way, that we could not
reach Newfoundland until the 7th of June.

The 8th of this month we entered into the Road
of St. John, where we found seventeen ships of
fishers. While we made somewhat long abode here,
Jaques Carthier and his company, returning from
Canada, whither he was sent with five sails the

year before, arrived in the very same harbour. Who after he had done his duty to our General, told him he had brought certain diamonds, and a quantity of gold ore, which was found in the country; which ore the Sunday next ensuing was tried in a furnace and found to be good.

Farthermore, he informed our General that he could not with his small company withstand the savages, which went about daily to annoy him, and this was the cause of his return into France. Nevertheless, he and his company commended the country to be very rich and fruitful. But when our General, being furnished with sufficient forces, commanded him to go back again with him, he and his company, moved as it seemed with ambition, because they would have all the glory of the discovery of those parts themselves, stole privily away the next night from us, and without taking their leaves, departed home for Bretaigne.

We spent the greatest part of June in the harbour of St. John, partly in furnishing ourselves with fresh water, whereof we stood in very great need by the way, and partly in composing and taking up a quarrel between some of our countrymen and certain Portugals. At length, about the last of the aforesaid month, we departed hence and entered into the Grand Bay, and passed by the Isle of Ascension ·(Anticosti), and finally arrived four leagues westward of the Isle of Orleans. In this place we found a convenient harbor for our shipping, where we cast anchor, went ashore with our people and chose out a convenient place to fortify ourselves in, fit to command the main river, and of strong situation against all invasion of enemies. Thus, toward the end of

July, we brought our victuals and other munitions and provisions on shore, and began to travail in fortifying ourselves.

*Of the Fort of France-Roy, and that which was done there.*

Having described the beginning, the midst, and the end of the voyage made by Monsieur Roberval in the countries of Canada, Hochelaga, Saguenay, and other countries in the west parts, he sailed so far (as is declared in other books) that he arrived in the said country, accompanied with 200 persons, soldiers, mariners and common people, with all furniture necessary for a fleet. The said general at his first arrival built a fair fort, near and somewhat westward above Canada, which is very beautiful to behold, and of great force, situated upon an high mountain, wherein there were two courts of buildings, a great tower, and another of 40 or 50 feet long, wherein there were divers chambers, an hall, a kitchen, houses of office, cellars high and low, and near unto it were an oven and mills, and a stove to warm men in, and a well before the house. And the building was situate upon the great river of Canada, called France Prime, by Monsieur Roberval. There was also at the foot of the mountain another lodging, part whereof was a great tower of two stories high, two courts of good building, where at the first all our victuals, and whatsoever was brought with us was sent to be kept ; and near unto that tower there is another small river. In these two places, above and beneath, all the meaner sort was lodged.

And in the month of August, and in the beginning of September, every man was occupied in such work as each one was able to do. But the 14th of

September our aforesaid general sent back into
France two ships which had brought his furniture,
and he appointed for admiral Monsieur de Saine-
terre, and the other captain was Monsieur Guinecourt, to carry news unto the King, and to come
back unto him the year next ensuing, furnished
with victuals and other things, as it should please
the King; and also to bring news out of France how
the King accepted certain diamonds which were
sent him, and were found in this country.

After these two ships were departed, consideration
was had how they should do and how they might
pass out the winter in this place. First they took
a view of the victuals, and it was found they fell
out short; and they were scanted so that in each
mess they had but two loaves weighing a pound
a-piece, and half a pound of beef. They ate bacon
at dinner with half a pound of butter; and beef at
supper and about two handfuls of beans without
butter.

On the Wednesday, Friday and Saturday, they did
eat dry cod, and sometimes they did eat it green at
dinner with butter, and they ate of porpoises and
beans at supper

About that time the savages brought us great stores
of aloses (shad, or salmon trout), which is a fish
somewhat red like a salmon, to get knives and other
small trifles for them.

In the end many of our people fell sick of a certain disease in their legs, veins and stomach, so that
they seemed to be deprived of all their limbs, and
there died thereof about fifty.

Note, that the ice began to break up in April.

Monsieur Roberval used very good justice, and

8

punished every man according to his offence. One, whose name was Michael Gaillon, was hanged for his theft. John of Nantes was laid in irons and kept prisoner for his offence, and others also were put in irons, and divers were whipped, as well men as women ; by which means they lived in quiet.

### The Manners of the Savages.

To declare unto you the state of the savages. They are people of a goodly stature and well made, they are very white, but they are all naked ; and if they were apparelled as the French are, they would be as white and as fair ; but they paint themselves for fear of heat and sunburning.

Instead of apparel they wear skins upon them like mantles, and they have a small pair of breeches, wherewith they cover their privities, as well men as women. They have hosen and shoes of leather, excellently made ; and they have no shirts, neither cover they the head, but their hair is trussed up above the crown of their heads and plaited or braided. Touching their victuals they eat good meat but all unsalted, but they dry it, and afterwards they boil it, as well fish as flesh. They have no certain dwelling-place, and they go from place to place, as they think they may best find food, as aloses in one place, and other fish, salmons, sturgeons, mullets, furmullets, barz, carps, eels, pimpermeaux, and other fresh water fish, and store of porpoises. They feed also of stags, wild boars, bugles, porkespines, and store of other wild beasts ; and there is as great store of fowls as they can desire.

Touching their bread, they make very good ; and

it is of great mill ; and they live very well ; for they take care for nothing else.

They drink seal oil, but this at their great feasts.

They have a king in every country, and are wonderful obedient unto him ; and they do him honour according to their manner and fashion. And when they travel from place to place, they carry all their goods with them in their boats.

The women nurse the children with the breast, and they sit continually, and are wrapped about the bellies with skins of fur.

*The voyage of Monsieur Roberval from his fort in Canada into Saguenay, the 5th June, 1543.*

Monsieur Roberval, the King's lieutenant in the countries of Canada, Saguenay and Hochelaga, departed toward the said province of Saguenay on the Tuesday, the 5th day of June, 1543, after supper ; and he with all his furniture was embarked to make the said voyage But upon a certain occasion they lay in the road over against the place before mentioned ; but on the Wednesday, about six o'clock in the morning, they set sail, and sailed against the stream, in which voyage their whole furniture was of eight barks, as well great as small, and to the number of three score and ten persons, with the aforesaid general.

The general left behind him in the aforesaid place and fort thirty persons to remain there until his return from Saguenay, which he appointed to be the first of July, or else they should return into France. And he left there behind him but two barks to carry the said thirty persons, and the furniture which was there, while he staid still in the country. And for

effectuating hereof, he left as his lieutenant a gentleman named Monsieur de Royeze, to whom he gave
commission, and charged all men to obey him, and
to be at the commandment of the said lieutenant.
The victuals which were left for their maintenance
until the said first day of July were received by the
said Lieutenant Royeze.

On Thursday, the 14th June, Monsieur l'Espiney,
La Brosse, Monsieur Frete, Monsieur Longeval and
others, returned from the general, from the voyage of
Saguenay.

And note, that eight men and one bark were
drowned and lost, amongst whom was Monsieur de
Feire Fontaine, and one named La Vasseur of Con-
sance.

On Tuesday, the 19th of June aforesaid, there
came from the general, Monsieur de Villeneuf, Tale-
bot, and three others, which brought six score pounds
weight of their corn, and letters to stay yet until
Magdalen-tide, which is the 22nd day of July.

[The rest of this voyage is wanting.]

*Here followeth the course from Belle Isle, Carpont, and the
Grand Bay, in Newfoundland, up the river of Canada, for
the space of 230 leagues, observed by Jean Alphonse of
Xainctoigne, chief pilot to Monsieur Roberval, 1542.*

Belles Isles are in 51 degrees and 40 min.; Belles
Isles and Carpont are N.N.W. and S.S.E. and they
are ten leagues distant; Carpont is in 52 deg.; Carpont and Belle Isle, from the Grand Bay, are N.E.
and S.W., and the distance from Belle Isle to the
Grand Bay is seven leagues. The midst of the Grand
Bay is in 52 deg. and a half, and on the north side

thereof there is a rock ; half a league from the isle, over against Carpont, toward the east, there is a small flat island, and on the side towards the N.E. there is a flat rock. And when thou comest out of the harbor of Carpont, thou must leave this rock on the starboard side, and also on the larboard side there are two or three small isles ; and when thou comest out of the N.E. side, ranging along the shore towards the west, about two pikes lengths in the midway, there is a shoal which lyeth on the starboard side ; and sail there by the north coast, and leave two parts of the Grand Bay towards the south, because there is a rock which runneth two or three leagues into the sea. And when thou art come athwart the haven of Butes, run along the north shore about one league or an half off, for the coast is without all danger. Belle Isle, in the mouth of the Grand Bay, and the Isles of Blanc Sablon, which are within the Grand Bay, near unto the north shore, lie N.E., W., and S. W., and the distance is 30 leagues. The Grand Bay at the entrance is but seven leagues broad from land to land, until it come over against the Bay des Chasteaux, and from thenceforward it hath not past five leagues in breadth ; and against Blanc Sablon it is eight leagues broad from land to land. And the land on the south shore is all low land along the sea coast ; the north shore is reasonable high land. Blanc Sablon is in 51 deg. 40 min. The Isles of Blanc Sablon and the Isles de la Demoiselle are N.E., W.S.W. and take a little of the W.S.W. and they are distant 36 leagues. These isles are in 50 deg. 45 min., and there is a good haven, and you may enter by an high cape which lyeth along toward the N.E., and within the distance of a pike and a half, because of a rock which lyeth on your larboard side, and you may anchor in ten fathom water over against a little nock, and from the great headland unto the place where thou doest anchor, there is not above the length of two cables. And if thou wouldst go out by the west side, thou must sail near the isle by the starboard, and give room unto the isle upon the larboard at the coming forth, and when thou art not past a cable's length out thou must sail hard by the isles on the larboard side, by reason of a sunken flat that lyeth on the starboard, and thence shalt sail on to the S.S.W. until thou come in sight of a rock which shineth, which is about half a league in the sea distant from the isles, and thou shalt leave it on the larboard (and from the Isles of Damoiselle unto Newfoundland, the sea is not in breadth above 36 leagues, because that Newfoundland, even unto Cape Breton, runneth not but N.N.E. and S.S.W.).

Between the Isles de la Demoiselle and the Isles of Blanc Sablon, there be many isles and good harbors; and on this coast there are falcons and hawks, and certain fowls which seem to be pheasants. The Isles de la Demoiselle and Cape Tienot are N.E. and S.S.W. and take a little of the N.E. and S.W., and they are distant 18 leagues. Cape Tienot is in 50 deg. 15 min., and there the sea is broadest. And it may be to the end of Newfoundland, which is at the entrance of Cape Briton, 70 leagues, which is the greatest breadth of this sea. And there are six or seven isles, between the Isles de la Demoiselle, and Cape Tienot.

Cape Tienot hath in the sea, five or six leagues distant from it, a sunken island, dangerous for ships.

The Cape Tienot and the midst of the Island of Ascension are N.E. and S.S.W., and they are 22 leagues distant; the midst of the Island of Ascension is in 49 deg. and a half. The said isle lyeth N.W. and S.E., the N.W. end is in 50 deg. of latitude, and the S.E. end is in 48 deg. and a half, and is about 25 leagues long, and four or five leagues broad; and from the N.W. end of the isle unto the firm land of the north side, the sea is not above seven leagues broad, and unto the firm land on the south side are about 15 leagues. Cape Tienot and the Isle of Ascension toward the S.E. are N.E. and S W., and are distant 30 leagues.

The said Cape of Tienot and the N.W. end of the Isle of Ascension are east and west, and take a little of the N.E. and S.W., and they are distant 34 leagues.

The Isle of Ascension is a goodly isle and a good champaigne land, without any hills, standing all upon white rocks and alabaster, all covered with trees unto the sea shore, and there are all sorts of trees as there be in France, and there be wild beasts, as bears, luserns, porkespicks. And from the S.E. end of the Isle of Ascension unto the entrance of Cape Breton is but 50 leagues. The N.W. end of the isle and the Cape des Monts nostre Dame, which is on the main land towards the south, are N.E. and W.S.W., and the distance between them is 15 leagues. The Cape is in 49 degrees, which is a very high land. The Cape end of the Isle of Ascension towards the S.E. are E. and W., and there is 15 leagues distance between them.

The Bay of Molues or Gaspay is in 48 degrees, and the coast lyeth north and south, and taketh a quarter of the N.E. and S.W. unto the Bay of Heate; and there are three isles, one great one and two small. From the Bay of Heate until you pass the Monts nostre Dame all the land is high and good ground, all covered with trees. Oguedoc is a good bay and lyeth N.N.W. and S.S.E., and it is a good harbour; and you must sail along the shore on the north side, by reason of the low point at the entrance thereof, and when you are past the point bring yourself to an anchor in 15 or 20 fathoms of water towards the south shore; and here within this haven are two rivers, one which goeth toward the N.W. and the other to the S.W. And on this coast there is great fishing for cods and other fish, where there is more store than is in Newfoundland, and better fish. And here is great store of river fowl, as mallards, wild geese, and others; and here are all sorts of trees, rose trees, raspberries, filbert trees, apple trees, pear trees, and it is hotter here in summer than in France.

The Isle of Ascension and the Seven Isles which lie on the north shore lie S.E. and W.S.W. and are distant 24 leagues. The Cape of Oguedoc and the Seven Isles are N.N.W. and S.S.E and are distant 35 leagues. The Cape of Monts nostre Dame and the Seven Islands are north and south, and the cut from one over to the other is 25 leagues, and this is the breadth of this sea and from thence upward it beginneth to wax narrower and narrower. The Seven Islands are in 50 degrees and a half. The Seven Islands and the Point of Ongear lie N.E. and S.W., and the distance between them is 15 leagues, and between them are certain small islands. And the point of Ongear and the Mountains nostre Dame, which are on the south side of the entrance of the river, are north and south, and the cut over from the one to the other is ten leagues, and this is here the breadth of the sea. The Point of Ongear and the river of Caen lie east and west, and they are distant 12 leagues. And all the coast from the Isle of Ascension hither is very good ground, wherein grow all sorts of trees that are in France, and some fruits. The Point of Ongear is 49 deg. and 15 min., and the River of Caen and the Isle of Raquelle lie N.E. and S.W., and they are distant 12 leagues. The Isle of Raquelle is in 48 deg. and 40 min. In this River of Caen there is great store of fish; and here the sea is not past eight league broad.

The Isle of Raquelle is a very low isle, which is near unto the south shore, hard by a high cape, which is called the Cape of Marble. There is no danger there at all, and between Raquelle and the Cape of Marble, ships may pass; and there is not from the isle to the south shore above one league, and from the isle to the north shore about four leagues. The Isle of Raquelle and the entrance of Saguenay are N.E. and W.S.W., and are distant 14 leagues, and there are between them two small islands near the north shore. The entrance of Saguenay is in 48 deg. and 20 min., and the entrance hath not past a quarter of a league in breadth, and it is dangerous toward the S.W., and two or three leagues within the entrance it beginneth to wax wider and wider, and it seemeth to be as it were an arm of the sea; and I think that the same runneth into the sea of Cathay, for it sendeth forth there a great current, and there doth run in that place a terrible race or tide. And here the river from the north shore is not past four leagues in breadth, and it is a dangerous passage between both the lands, because there lie banks of rocks in the river.

The Isle of Raquelle and the Isle of Hares lie N.E. and S.W., and take a quarter of the east and west, and they are distant 18 leagues. The entrance of Saguenay and the Isle of Hares lie N.N.E. and S.S.W., and are distant five leagues. The entrance of Saguenay and the Isle of Raquelle are N.N.W. and S.S.W., and are distant three leagues. The Isle of Hares is in 48 deg. 4 min. From the Mountains of notre Dame unto Canada and unto Hochelaga, all the land on the south coast is fair, a low land and goodly champaigne, all covered with trees unto the bank of the river. And the land on the north side is higher, and in some places there are high mountains. And from the Isle of Hares unto the Isle of Orleans the river is not past four or five leagues broad. Between the Isle of Hares and the high land on the north side the sea is not past a league and a half broad, and it is very deep, for it is above 100 fathoms deep in the midst. To the east of the Isle of Hares and the Isle of Filberts lie N.E., W., and S.W., and they are distant 12 leagues. And you must always run along the high land on the north shore, for on the other shore there is nothing but rocks; and you must pass by the side of the Isle of Filberts, and the River there is not past a quarter of a league broad, and you must sail in the midst of the channel, and in the midst runneth the best passage either at an high or low water, because the sea runneth there strongly, and there are great dangers of rocks, and you had need of good anchor and cable. The Isle of Filberts is a small isle, about one league long, and half a league broad, but they are all banks of sand.

The Isle of Filberts stands in 47 deg. 45 min. The Isle of Filberts and the Isle of Orleans lie N.E. and S.W., and they are distant ten leagues, and thou must pass by the high land on the north side, about a quarter of a league, because that in the midst of the river there is nothing but shoals and rocks. And when thou shalt be over against a round cape, thou must take over to the south shore S.W. ¼ S, and thou shalt sail in five, six, and seven fathoms; and there the river of Canada beginneth to be fresh, and the salt water endeth. And when thou shalt be athwart the point of the Isle of Orleans, where the river beginneth to be fresh, thou shalt sail in the midst of the river, and thou shalt leave the isle on the starboard, which is on the right hand ; and here the river is not past a quarter of a league broad, and hath 20 and 30 fathoms water. And toward the south shore there is a ledge of isles all covered with trees, and they end over against the point of the Isle of Orleans. And the point of the Isle of Orleans toward the N.E. is in 47 deg. 20 min. And the Isle of Orleans is a fair isle, all covered with trees even unto the river side ; and it is about five leagues long and a league and a half broad. And on the north shore there is another river, which falleth into the main river at the end of the island ; and ships may very well pass there. From the midst of the isle unto Canada the river runneth west, and from the place of Canada unto France Roy the river runneth W.S.W., and from the west end of the isle to Canada is but one league, and unto France Roy four leagues ; and when thou art come to the end of the isle, thou shalt see a great river which falleth 15 or 20 fathoms down from a rock, and maketh a terrible noise. The fort of France Roy is in 47 deg, 10 min.

The extension of all these lands, upon just occasion, is called NEW FRANCE, for it is as good and as temperate as France, and in the same latitude. And the reason wherefore it is colder in winter is because the fresh river is naturally more cold than the sea; and it is also broad and deep; and in some places it is half a league and above in breadth; and also because the land is not tilled nor full of people; and it is all full of woods, which is the cause of cold, because there is not store of fire nor cattle. And the sun hath its meridian as high as the meridian at Rochel, and it is noon here, when the sun is at S.S.W. at Rochel. And here the north star by the compass standeth N.N.E., and when at Rochel it is noon, it is but half an hour past nine at France Roy.

From the said place unto the ocean sea and coast of New France is not above 50 leagues' distance, and from the entrance of Norumbega unto Florida are 300 leagues: and from this place of France Roy to Hochelaga are about 80 leagues, and unto the isle of Rasus 30 leagues. And I doubt not but Norumbega entereth into the river of Canada, and unto the sea of Saguenay. And from the fort of France Roy until a man come forth of the Grand Bay is not above 230 leagues: and the course is N.E. and W.S.W., not above five deg. and 20 min. difference, and reckon 16 leagues and a half to a degree.

By the nature of the climate the lands towards Hochelaga are still better and better, and more fruitful; and this land is fit for figs and pears; and I think that gold and silver will be found here, according as the people of the country say. These lands lie over against Tartary, and I doubt not but they stretch toward Asia, according to the roundness of the world. And, therefore, it were good to have a small ship of 70 tons to discover the coast of New France on the back side of Florida; for I have been at a bay as far as 42 degrees between Norumbega and Florida, and I have not searched the end thereof, and I know not whether it pass through. And in all these countries there are oaks, and bortz, ashes, elm, arables, trees of life, pines, prusse trees, cedars, great walnut trees, and wild nuts, hazel trees, wild pear trees, wild grapes, and there have been found red plums. And very fair corn groweth there, and peason grow of their own accord, gooseberries and strawberries. And there are goodly forests wherein men may hunt; and there are great store of stags, deer, porkepicks, and the savages say there be unicorns. Fowl there are in abundance, as bustards, wild geese, cranes, turtle doves, ravens, crows, and many other birds. All things which are sown there are not past two or three days in coming up out of the ground. I have told in one ear of corn 120 grains, like the corn of France. And you need not to sow your wheat until March, and it will be ripe in the midst of August. The waters are better and perfecter than in France, and if the country were tilled and replenished with people, it would be as hot as Rochel. And the reason why it snoweth oftener there than in France is because it raineth there but seldom; for the rain is converted into snows. All things above mentioned are true.

John Alphonse made this voyage with Monsieur Roberval.

A.W. Moore
del.

# THE FOURTH VOYAGE.

*Some time after March 25, 1543, Cartier was sent back to get Roberval, which he did, returning at the end of eight months.*

[See Lescarbot, ed. 1612, page 416 : "Car je trouve par le compte du dit Quartier qu'il employa huit mois à l'aller quèrir après y avoir demeure dix-sept mois." See Transactions Quebec Literary and Historical Society, 1862, p. 93.]

This voyage has of late been held by some to have never been made, and the most recent authority on Cartier (Longrais), is of this opinion. All that can be said at present is that it is a matter of opinion.

After he had retired from the sea, he occupied during the winter, in the town of St. Malo, a house situated "next St. Thomas' Hospital," of which nothing now remains. There is or was a street in St. Malo, named after him. During the summer he withdrew to the seignorial domain of Limoilou, at the village of the same name. In an Act of the Chapitre of St. Malo, of the 29th September, 1549, he was made Sieur de Limoilou, and it is claimed, on the 5th February following, was made a noble. After the return of Roberval, he had to undergo an examination as to the expenditure of money. He was acquitted on all charges by the sentences of the tribunal of the Admiralty on the 21st June, 1544.

On the 21st October, 1542, Cartier was present at a baptism in St. Malo, of the daughter of the Governor. He was also at a baptism on the 25th March, 1543, Easter; on the 6th August, 1544; 27th April, 1547; 8th December, 1547; 20th December, 1548; and others, the last one recorded being on the 17th November, 1555.

On the 10th April, 1543, Cartier was chosen interpreter of Portuguese, another evidence that he had been in the Portuguese employ. On the 17th December, 1544, he is called upon to give testimony in a marine enquiry instituted by order of the King. In 1545 he gives evidence in small cases before a magistrate, and also during the years 1546 and 1548.

On April 3, 1544, he and Roberval are summoned to appear before the King, with the result as stated above.

According to l'Abbé Manet, on the 29th November, 1549, Cartier and his wife founded an obit in the Cathedral of St. Malo ; and Longrais has discovered the book of obits of the cathedral, in which Cartier and his wife are inscribed for a simple obit of three masses on the 16th of October of each year.

It may be of interest to state that the account runs that Roberval made a voyage in 1549 and never came back. The proof is to the effect that he was assassinated in Paris.

On Sunday, 17th of September, 1553, " a savage of the countries of the New Land " was baptized, but Cartier did not act as godfather. The fact shows that voyages were kept up.

On Tuesday, the 5th of June, 1555, Cartier appears as a bond-giver in a *tutelle*. On the 16th June, 1556, Cartier's name appears as a witness, and also on

Friday, the 17th of July, and again on the 27th November, in small cases.

And now the end approaches; the great navigator is going on the eternal voyage, and on the 1st September, 1557, he set sail for the celestial world. On the margin of one of the precious registers of St. Malo, only recently come to light, his passing away is thus recorded: "Ce dict mercredy au matin environ cinq heures deceda Jacques Cartier." "On the said Wednesday, about five o'clock in the morning, died Jacques Cartier." A plague or epidemic was raging in the district, and Cartier probably fell a victim.

And he had no son to follow in his work, so that his mantle fell on Champlain half a century later.

There are two portraits of Cartier, one in the city hall of St. Malo, and one in the National Library at Paris. The former is familiar to many, as there are many copies and prints of it, one of which is to be found in the first volume of "Histoire de la Colonie Française," by Faillon. A reproduction of the other is to be found on the title page of "Note sur le Manoir de Jacques Cartier, par M. Alfred Rame," Paris, 1867.

[Hakluyt, in the third volume, gives the two following letters. They are to be found immediately after the third voyage of Cartier.]

*A Letter written to M. John Growte, student in Paris, by Jaques Noel, of S. Malo, the nephew of Jaques Cartier, touching the foresaid discovery.*

Master Growte, your brother-in-law, Giles Walter, shewed me this morning a map printed at Paris, dedicated to one M. Hakluyt, an English gentleman, wherein all the West Indies, the kingdom of New Mexico, and the countries of Canada, Hochelaga and

9

Saguenay are contained. I hold that the river of
Canada, which is described in that map, is not marked
as it is in my book, which is agreeable to the book of
Jacques Cartier; and that the said chart doth not
mark or set down The Great Lake, which is above
the saults, according as the savages have advertised
us, which dwell at the said saults. In the foresaid
chart, which you sent me hither, the Great Lake is
placed too much toward the north. The saults or
falls of the river stand in 44 degrees of latitude; it
is not so hard a matter to pass them as it is thought.
The water falleth not down from any high place, it
is nothing else but that in the midst of the river
there is bad ground. It were best to build boats
above the saults; and it is easy to march or travel
by land to the end of the three saults; it is not
above five leagues' journey. I have been upon the
top of a mountain, which is at the foot of the saults.
where I have seen the said river beyond the said
saults, which shewed unto us to be broader than it
was where we passed it. The people of the country
advertised us that there are ten days' journey
from the sault into this great lake. We know not
how many leagues they make to a day's journey.
At this present I cannot write unto you more at
large, because the messenger can stay no longer.
Here, therefore, for the present I will end, saluting
you with my hearty commendations, praying God
to give you your heart's desire. From S. Malo, in
haste, this 19th day of June, 1587.

Your loving friend,

JAQUES NOEL.

Cousin, I pray you do me so much pleasure as to send me a book of the discovery of New Mexico, and one of those new maps of the West Indies dedicated to M. Hakluyt, the English gentleman, which you sent to your brother-in-law, Giles Walter. I will not fail to inform myself if there be any mean to find out those descriptions which Captain Cartier made after his two last voyages into Canada.

*Underneath the aforesaid imperfect relation that which followeth is written in another Letter sent to M. John Growte, student in Paris, from Jaques Noel of S. Malo, the Grand-Nephew of Jaques Cartier.*

I can write nothing else unto you of anything that I can recover of the writings of Captain Jaques Cartier, my uncle, deceased, although I have made search in all places that I possibly could in this town; saving of a certain book made in manner of a sea-chart, which was drawn by the hand of my said uncle, which is in the possession of Master Cremeur, which book is passing well marked and drawn, for all the river of Canada, whereof I am well assured, because I myself have knowledge thereof, as far as to the saults, where I have been; the height of which sault is in 44 degrees. I found in the said chart, beyond the place where the river is divided in twain, in the midst of both the branches of the said river, somewhat nearest that area which runneth toward the N.W., these words following, written in the hand of Jaques Cartier:—"By the people of Canada it was said, that here is the land of Saguenay, which is rich and wealthy in precious stones." And about one hundred leagues under the same, I found written these two lines following in the said card, inclining toward the S. W.: "Here in this country are cinnamon and cloves, which they call in their language, Canodeta." Touching the effect of my book, whereof I spake unto you, it is made after the manner of a sea-chart, which I have delivered unto my two sons, Michael and John, which at this present are in Canada. If, at their return, which will be, God willing, about Magdalentide, they have learned any new thing worthy the writing, I will not fail to advertise you thereof.

Your loving friend,

Jaques Noel.

# NOTES.

## FIRST VOYAGE.

[The dates given are in the " old style" of reckoning. In France the " old style" prevailed until 1582, in England till 1752.]

*Cartier.*—Lescarbot spells this uniformly Quartier, and is followed by the Literary and Historical Society of Quebec. The majority of authorities and writers, as well as usage, commend the former method. The writer is of the opinion that the letter *C* is intended. See autograph.

Ramusio has " armate ciascuna." Lescarbot says " armé de soixante-et-un hommes." The Rev. B. F. DaCosta says the ships were about fifty tons each, and were manned with 162 chosen men. Ramusio and Lescarbot both say sixty tons, "sixty-one men each." Faillon says sixty-one in all. Ramusio says sixty-one in each, so Hakluyt. DaCosta says 162 men.

*Newfoundland.*—The name *Terra Nova* and *Terre Neuve* was given on all the old maps to the whole of the northern region of this continent, and in a statute of Henry VIII. is named "Newland." It has, of course, not the same meaning at present, being applied to only an inconsiderable portion. Verazzano gave the name of *Terre Neuve* to·Florida (Lescarbot).

Cabot was and should be, apart from fishermen, accredited as the discoverer of *Baccalaos* (land of codfish) or Newfoundland. DeBry. *Grand Voyages,* iv., p. 69. Belle-forest. *Cosmographie Universelle,* tome 11, 2175, published at Paris, 1576. *Du Nouveau Monde, Chauveton,* page 141, Geneva, 1579. *Singularité de la France Antartique, Thevet.* Cabot made a map of these coasts, Labrador, where he first touched, and further north. He gave names to points in Hudson's Bay. It must not be forgotten that, by the right of discovery,

America belonged to the English nation, for Cabot saw the continent fourteen months before Columbus.

Savages brought from the " Newfound Iland" were shown in England in 1502. (Purchas, page 915, ed. 1617.) See additional note.

*Cape de Bonne-veue.*—Capo di Buona Vista. *Ramusio.* Bonavista.

*Golfe St. Lunaire.*—Lescarbot says this is *Tregate.*

*Longitude.* \* \* \* \*—*Ramusio* does not give it. In those days longitude was reckoned from Ferro, supposed to be the most western part of the world, and " proceeded first over the old world and thus made its journey of 360 degrees."

*League.*—Equal to about 3.052 statute miles.

*Island of Birds.*—Funk Island.

*Apporrath,*—Lescarbot has Apponath. " The Acadians call them Barricadières. ' "

*Newfoundland.*—In an edition of Ptolemy, published at Bâsle, 1540, is a map " Typus Orbis Universalis," in which is seen in the extreme north of the new world, " Terra Nova siva Bacalhos," and below it to the southward is an island designated " Corterati," with a great stream in its rear (the St. Lawrence *perhaps*), thus characterised " Per hoc fretum iterpated ad Molucas." (A copy of this map is in the Harvard College Library.)

*Godetz, Margaulx.*—Lescarbot has *godets, margaux.* The godets are probably godwits. " Now known as godes." Godes means sea-birds.

*Castle Gulf.*—Golfe des Châteuaulx, Lescarbot. Golfo di Castelli, Ramusio. Straits of Belle Isle.

*Degrad.*—Or " De Grat."

*Carpunt.*—Carpont. Ramusio. 51°N.

*Cape Race.*—Capo rasso. Ramusio. Cap Razé. Lescarbot.

*Isle Ste. Catherine.*—Island of Belle Isle.

*Castle Harbor.*—Port des Châteaux. Lescarbot. Porto di Castelli. Ramusio.

*Port des Gouttes.*—Baie Verte, Labrador.

*Port des Balances.*—Porto dello ballanze. Ramusio. Baie Royal, Labrador.

*Blanc-Sablon.*—Bianco Sabbione. Ramusio.

*Isle de Brest.*—Isle au Bois, Labrador.

*Les Ilettes.*—L'Isolette. Ramusio. " Havre de Labrador."

*Isle des Oiseaux.*—Isle Verte, Labrador.

*Longitude * * *.*—Not given by Ramusio.

*Duck's Eggs.*—"These are the eggs of a bird called Moignac, by the *voyageurs* of Labrador."

*Port Brest, Saint Servan.*—Breton names of places; now Baie du Vieux Fort, and Rocky Bay.

*Port Jacques Cartier.*—Shecatica Bay.

*River St. James.*—Bay of Nepetepick.

*St. Antoine.*—Lobster Bay, or Baie des Homards.

*Oven.*—Forno, Ramusio. Fourneau, Lescarbot.

*Boul tree.*—Lescarbot says it is similar to the oak. It is the birch.

*Cape Double.*—Now la pointe Riche, Newfoundland.

*Cape Pointed.*—Capo puntito. Ramusio. Now Cow Head.

*Hut Mountains.*—Monti delle grange. Ramusio. Montagnes des cabannes, south of Bay Ingomachoix, on the west coast of Nova Scotia.

As Cartier was married to Catherine des Granches, the mountains were in all probability, named thus, and the name given by Ramusio is an error. Lescarbot.

*Pigeon House Islands.*—Dell'Isole Columbare. Ramusio. Lescarbot calls them Isles Ramées.

*Fifteenth.*—Lescarbot has twenty-fifth—an error.

*Cape St. John.*—Now Cap de l'Auguille, (Eel Cape.)

*Brion Island.*—Named after the Admiral who was patron of the expedition. This is said by Dr. Kohl, in his *Discovery of Maine,* (p. 326), to be Prince Edward Island.

*Goose.*—Oche. Ramusio. Oysons. Lescarbot. (Goslings.)

*Islands of Margaux.*—Da Costa says these are the Bird Islands.

*I think there is a channel, etc.*—There is some doubt as to the correctness of this text. The *Relation originale* quoted by Da Costa, says: "Between the new land and the land of the Bretons." Lescarbot says at page 274, ed. 1612, speaking of Jacques Cartier, " ne sachant pas au vray qu'il y eut passage par le Cap-Breton," *i.e.*, not knowing the fact that there was a channel by way of Cape Breton. See last chapter of Second Voyage.

*Gulf St. Julien.*—Bonne Baie.

*Cape Royal.*—Cape Nord de la Baie des Isles.

*Cape Milk.*—Pointe Sud de la Baie des Isles.

*Alezay.*—This is presumed to be what is now known as Prince Edward Island ; or, it may be one of the Magdalen Islands.

*Canoe River, Rivière des Barques.*—Fiume delle barche. Ramusio. Now Miramichi river.

*Cape St. Peter.*—A cape of one of the Magdalen Islands.

* * * * *of width, etc.*—A hiatus here in Ramusio.

*Castle Gulf.*—Straits of Belle-Isle.

" *Napeu tondamen assurtah.*"—Belle-forest translates this: " We wish to have your friendship," on which Lescarbot remarks, " I do not know where he got this, but to-day (*i.e.* circa, 1600), they do not speak thus."

*Hatchets.*—Ramusio has " manerette," which is given in the Indian vocabulary at end of Second Voyage. In another place "manerettes" of tin are spoken of, these could hardly be hatchets. Probably trinkets is the proper word.

*Warmer than Spain.*—Lescarbot says : " The author has equivocated, or has wished to make a standing rule from a single experience of heat, because the Gulf (Bay of Chaleur) being 48½° cannot be so warm, in that country at least. The Indian name was Mowebaktabääk, or the Biggest Bay.

*Wild wheat.*—Vetches perhaps.

*Capo di Prato.*—Cap du Pré. Lescarbot. Now Cape Farillon. It may simply mean Cape Meadow, otherwise a curious interest centres about this name. It is stated to have been named after Albert de Prato, who wrote a letter from Newfoundland to Cardinal Wolsey, addressed " Reverend in Christo Patri Domino Cardinali et Domino Legato Angliæ." The date is " apud le Baya Saint Johan in Terris Novis die X Augusti 1527. Revr. Patr. vest. humilis, servus Albertus de Prato." He was probably Canon of St. Paul's. Those interested may find this letter in Purchas (vol. iii., p. 809), together with one from John Rut. One writer, D'Avezac, claims that this Albert de Prato was the *piemontais* massacred by the savages, whereas there is much stronger reason for believing that this *pilot piemontais* was none other than Verrazani. (See note " De Prato.) Consult *Memoir of Cabot*, pp. 273, 278.

*Above and across their bodies.*—Lescarbot has it, " à la mode des Egyptiens."

*Our captain.*—Cartier. He is thus spoken of in the first and second voyages.

*Grain as large as peas.*—Mil ou mahis, Lescarbot; del miglio, Ramusio. Indian corn. Compare mahis and maize. (See note under " large grain," 2nd voyage.)

*Kapaige*—Lescarbot notes that the language has changed since the time of Cartier.

*Twenty-fourth.*—Lescarbot has it, first of August.

*Fifteen leagues.*—Lescarbot has it, sixteen.

*Straits St. Pierre.*—Between Anticosti and Gaspé. Da Costa says, they were between Anticosti and Labrador (an error.)

*Cape Tiennot.*—Cape Montjoli; near here is the river Natachquoin.

*5th September.*—Da Costa says the 1st, but gives no authority.

---

### SECOND VOYAGE.

The bishop who blessed them on leaving was "le vénérable Denis Briconnet."

*Fourteen leagues from mainland.*—Ramusio has it forty-four.

*Eight o'clock in the evening.*—Ramusio has it, till half-past one.

*Havre St. Nicholas.*—Mingan.

*Cape Tiennot.*—Cape Mountjoli.

*Two reefs.*—Lescarbot has it, four.

*Seventh of August.*—Lescarbot has 8th; two manuscripts 8th, one 7th; Ramusio, 7th.

*Bay of St. Lawrence.*--St. John river (on the Labrador coast?); the name afterwards given to the present Gulf and river. Gomara, writing in 1555, says: "It has been navigated two hundred leagues up, on which account many call it the Straits of the Three Brothers. Here the water forms a square Gulf, which extends from San Lorenço to the point of Baccallaos, more than two hundred leagues."

*Twelfth of August.*—Ramusio 12th, two manuscripts 13th, one 14th; Lescarbot 14th.

*Assumption Island.*—Anticosti at present. Indian name, Natiscotec. Jean Allefonce persists in calling it Ascension Island.

*High Lands.*—Gaspé; old name Gachepé.

*Sileune de Hochelaga.*—"Fiume" in Ramusio; fleuve in Lescarbot.

*Shaped like a horse.*—Lescarbot calls them, "hippopotanie or river horses."

*St. John Islands.*—Lescarbot calls them, *Le Pic.* Bic Islands.

*Canada.*—The origin of this word is, and probably ever will be, a matter of dispute. Dean Trench has said its origin and meaning are unknown—a hasty conclusion. Amongst others given are the expressions, *Aca-nada* (nothing here), *Cabo de nada* (Cape Nothing) and *que nada da* (yielding nothing), which were used by the Basques. Also, *Cannata* or *Kannata*, an Iroquois term for a collection of huts. Compare the expression in the Indian vocabulary at the end of the second voyage, *Canada-undagneny* (where do you come from?) In this case, the actual word Canada is found in print in 1545 and 1556; tending to prove it to be an Indian word. These are the first times this word is found in print, I believe. Lescarbot writes of the word *Canada* as follows :—It is properly the name of both banks of that large river, to which has been given the name of Canada, * * *. Others have called the river Hochelaga, the name of a district above the Croix, where Jacques Cartier wintered. The people of Gachepé (Gaspé), of the Bay of Chaleur * * * call themselves *Canadocœa*, that is Canadaquois (as we say Iroquois, etc.), and he goes on to say that the name of the river should be the River of Canada, rather than Hochelaga or St. Lawrence, and that the country on both sides of the river is Canada. "This word Canada, (he continues) being properly the name of a province, I cannot agree with Belle-forest, who says it means land, nor with Captain Jacques Cartier, who says it means a town (ville). I believe both are mistaken, and that their mistake was due to the fact that, speaking to these tribes by means of signs, some one of the French asked the savages how (by what name) they called their country, pointing to one of their villages, or circle of ground, they replied that it was Canada, not meaning their village or ground was called thus, but the whole country." Garneau says in his *Histoire du Canada*, that Canada means a collection of huts.

When Canada is spoken of by Cartier, it is to be applied only to that part commencing above Isle aux Coudres at the Island of Orleans, and extending to Hochelaga. The other portions of this new country were named Saguenay, Honguedo, Hochelaga. Saguenay was the district from the Gulf to Isle aux Coudres; Hochelaga was the district about the present site of Montreal; while Honguedo was applied to that district now known as Gaspé.

*Two savages * * * preceding voyage.*—There is mention of a chief's sons.

*One of these islands is ten leagues long.*—The Island of Orleans, at first called the Isle of Bacchus by Cartier, and then changed by him to its present name in honor of the Duc d'Orleans. It also bore the name of St. Laurent down to 1770 in public Acts; also called Baccalaos by LaHontau, Minigo by the Indians; and Isle de Ste. Marie and "Isle des Sorciers." There is a history of the island by Turcotte.

*Large grain.*—" For their seeds and graines, mays is principall, of which they make their bread, which our English ground brings forth, but will hardly ripen; it grows, as it were, on a reed and multiplyeth beyond comparison; they gather three hundred measures for one. It yeeldeth more bloud, but more grosse than our wheate. They make drinke thereof also, wherewith they will be exceedingly drunke; they first steep and after boyle it to that end. In some places they first cause it to bee champed with maids, in some places with olde women, and then make a leaven thereof, which they boyle and make this inebriating drinke. The canes and leaves serve for their mules to eat. They boyle and drinke it also for paine in the backe. The buds of mays serve instead of butter and oyle." *Purchas,* page 911, edition 1617, London.

*St. Croix.*—This is undoubtedly the River St. Charles. Efforts have been made to prove that Cartier wintered at the river now named after him, but without success at all. Throughout the first and second voyages the writer has given this name in his translation—a whim perhaps, but it is a pity that the name of St. Croix had not been retained. (See additional note, " Where Cartier wintered.")

*After we had returned, etc.*—Lescarbot here says, in effect, that the lateness of the season obliged Cartier to seek suitable winter quarters, finding himself in a distant land, in a river never before explored, which he was determined to do; for which reason he had not stopped at Saguenay, Isle aux Coudres, nor Orleans (where he put on shore the two savages brought back from France. He found a suitable place to winter, and went back to the island of Orleans to bring up the ships which he had left there.

*The island.*—Orleans.

*Taignoagny.*—Lescarbot has it, *Taguragny.*

*How Donnacona, etc.*—Why these people wished to prevent Cartier can be only accounted for by supposing that those at Hochelaga were their enemies, or that they wished to retain Cartier with them on account of the trinkets they were receiving, or perhaps these two suppositions combined were the reason.

*Cudriagny.*—Cudruaigni, Ramusio; Cudonagny, Lescarbot. This was their deity, concerning whom they had some very peculiar notions. Consult Lescarbot and others.

*Cornet.*—This is a shell, and the word is still in use.

*Ochelay.*—Ochelai, Ramusio; Achelaci, Lescarbot. This was probably near to the present site of Three Rivers. Champlain states this to have been fifteen leagues above Quebec. (See note, "Where Cartier wintered.")

*A large lake.*—Lake St. Peter.

*Four or five rivers.*—Sorel Islands; these "rivers" were the channels between the different islands.

*Fifteen leagues.*—Probably an error. The islands are only about that distance from Montreal.

*Second of October.*—19th, Ramusio; 19th, reprint; 2nd, manuscript.

*Forty-five leagues.*—This is full measure, with a vengeance.

*Half-a-league.*—The exact site of Hochelaga is a matter of doubt. The writer has dug up Indian relics on Peel street, Montreal. Consult Sir Wm. Dawson's paper in *Canadian Naturalist.* (See note, "The site of Hochelaga," in this volume. When Champlain visited the locality in 1603, the village and its dusky inhabitants had disappeared. This renders difficult credence in the theory that the relics found since 1860, near Sherbrooke street, were those of the Hochelagans.

*Huts or houses.*—Usually the "houses of savages * * * were nothing but poles set round and meeting in the top, ten foot broad, the fire in the middest, covered with deeres-skins." Purchas, 930, ed. 1617. "The savages dwell in houses made of fir trees, bound together in the top and set around like a dove-house, this * * * at the entry to the Gulf of St. Lawrence."

*Esurgny.*—Other names given are Enogny, Esuogny, and Esnogny. Lescarbot, speaking of this word (page 732, ed. 1612), says he had great difficulty in understanding it, and that Belle-forest did not understand it at all. To-day (he continues) they have none, or have lost the method of making (finding) it. They adorn themselves with trinkets from France, that is the women; they call these trinkets *Matachiaz.* At Port Royal, Newfoundland and Tadousac, they make use of the quills of the porcupine, which they dye black, white and red, etc. Sir William Dawson has tried to explain "esurgny."

*Some mystery.*—That is to give a historical representation or religious ceremony. These mysteries were probably frequent in France where Cartier had evidently seen them; they were given on special occasions, and the connection between them, miracle plays, and the stage, is a close one. Consult any good history of English literature, and consult the "Abbot," by Sir Walter Scott.

*Three months.*—The manuscripts have "leagues." Lescarbot and Ramusio have "months" (*lunes.*)

*Up the river.*—Lescarbot has an interpolation following this :—
"And I remember that Donnacona, chief of the Canadians, told us
he had visited a country, a month's journey distant from Canada, in
which grow cloves and cinnamon ; and cinnamon they call *adotathui,*
cloves *canonotha.*"

*A large river.*—A branch of the Ottawa, back of the island of
Montreal.

*Agouiandas.*—Agajoudas, Lescarbot; agouiondas, Ramusio.

*Caignet-daze.*—Caignedazé, Lescarbot.

*River of Faith.*—St. Maurice. Champlain gave it its present
name.

*How the savages, etc.*—This chapter and the following one are not
in Ramusio nor Lescarbot, but are in the three manuscripts.

*One more than ten leagues long.*—Orleans.

*Adhothuys.*—This has been asserted to be the *Beluga Catadon,* or
white whale, of which bones have been found in the post-pliocene
clay of the St. Lawrence.

*Fresh-water sea.*—Lake St. John ?

*Notre Dame de Roquemado.*—Lescarbot, page 376, says :—" Or to
call it more correctly, to Roque amadon, that is to say, of lovers. It
is a *bourg* of Querci, visited by many pilgrims."

*Ameda.*—*Anneda,* Lescarbot.

This remedy was made of the leaves and bark of *l'épinette blanche.*

*Stags.*—(*Daims*)  Moose or Caribou.

*Aiounesta.*—Ajounesta, Lescarbot.

*Leave one of our ships.*—Parts of this, it is claimed, were discovered
in 1843, and some of them sent to the Museum at St. Malo. (See
note, Remains of *La Petite Hermine.*)

*Charles Guyot.*—In Ramusio, and the reprint, Jehan Poullet is
mentioned as going with him.

*Agouhanna.*—Agona, Lescarbot; Agonna, Ramusio.

*White men.*—This is probably untrue. It might be referred to the
Eskimos.

*Picquemyans.*—Picqueniaux, Lescarbot; Picquemjans, Ramusio
and manuscripts.

*Licadin.*—Stadin in two manuscripts ; Litadin in one manuscript ;
Stadin in Lescarbot : Lidaten in Ramusio.

*The bottom of the ship.*—How does this agree with the finding of
certain portions of it in the year 1843 ?

*Canadians.*—This occurs "*ians*" in reprint, probably the first time in print of this word. Ramusio has *Canadiani* and *Canidiani.*

*Colliers.*—Lescarbot calls them *echarpes*, scarfs. These *colliers* were a favorite ornament of dress of Indians. In recent times those of the Rocky Mountains made them of the teeth of the grizzly bear, killed by the wearer, such *colliers* being considered an evidence of bravery and skill.

*Casnou.*—*Casnoui*, Ramusio; *caswini*, Lescarbot.

*Twenty-two leagues and a-half.*—Ramusio and reprint say two leagues and a half.

$46\frac{1}{2}°$.—Ramusio has $45\frac{1}{2}°$.

*Bay of the Holy Ghost.*—Port aux Basques.

*Two, three and four leagues out in the sea.*—Ramusio and the reprint say twenty-three leagues.

*Cap Torraine.*—Cap Nord, Cape Breton.

*Rognouse.*—Baie des Trépassés.

*Isles St. Pierre.*—St. Pierre de Miquelon.

*Cape St. Paul.*—This name appears on the map of Maijolla, 1527, and on that of Viegas, drawn in 1533. Now Cap d'Aspé.

*6th July.*—Da Costa states the date to have been the 1st July.

———

## THIRD VOYAGE.

The savages brought back on the second voyage by Cartier were Donnacona, Taiguragny, Domagaya, and seven others. The King ordered them to be religiously instructed, which was done in Bretagne. Cartier was godfather to one. Donnacona received the name of François. They lived for about four years, all dying except a little girl ten years old.

The date of departure of Cartier on his third voyage is given in Hakluyt and the Quebec Historical and Literary Society's volume, " Voyages *et decouvertes*, etc., Quebec, 1843," as the 23rd May, 1540. As Cartier only received his letters patent on the 17th October, 1540, this is a mistake for 1541. Roberval's account is that he himself set sail on the 16th April, 1542, and that Cartier had been sent the year previous, that is, in 1541. Faillon, in his *Histoire de la Colonie Française*, states that Cartier sailed on the 23rd May, 1541. This must be regarded as the correct date. See note further on: " Dates of the Third Voyage."

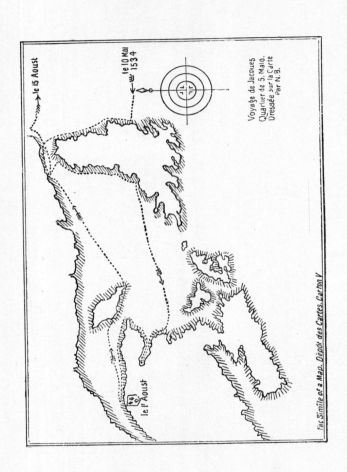

le 15 Aoust

le 10 Mai
1534

Voyage de Jacques
Quartier de S. Malo.
Dressée sur la Carte
Par N. B.

le l' Aoust

Fac Similie of a Map. Dépôt des Cartes. Carton V

The Rev. B F. Da Costa, D. D., author of the essay on Jacques Cartier, in the *Narrative History of America*, edited by Justin Winsor, states that Cartier took with him on his third voyage the " Grande Hermine" and the " Emerillon." In the commission given to Cartier (see note " Sieur de Roberval") it is distinctly stated that the latter vessel was old, and permission was granted to dismantle her, in order to aid in the equipment of the other vessels.

Thevet, in his *Cosmographie Universelle* (Paris, 1575), publishes a story of Roberval's neice being put ashore with her old nurse on the " Isle of Demons" (see Gastalde's map, published in this vol.), for becoming the victim of her lover. The latter was allowed to join them. Her nurse and her lover died. More than two years after she was taken home to France in a fishing vessel. The story was first told in the Heptameron of Marguerite (see *Narrative and Critical History of America*, vol. iv., page 66 ; and Transactions Royal Society of Canada, vol. i., page 40). Modern writers have used the incident, among them, I think, Frechette.

*Cartier's Route.*—Among the copies made by the late Ben Perley Poore for Parkman is a map of the St. Lawrence Gulf, with the route of Cartier in 1534 pricked out. The map is signed N. B., and is supposed to have been made by N. Bellin, the map-maker who supplied Charlevoix with his maps. Of this map, in answer to a query, Mr. Parkman writes me as follows :—" The map is in one of a collection of volumes of manuscripts given by me to the Massachusetts Historical Society, in whose library it now is. The map is a colored sketch, very small, and, in my opinion, of little value as authority. The points on the Gulf visited by Cartier in his first voyage are indicated on it, but it gives no new information." In another letter he says : " I send you a tracing of the Cartier * * * * the facsimile was made for me from the original in the Depot des Cartes de la Marine, Paris. F. PARKMAN."

*Captain Hore.*—At page 517 of Hakluyt's *Principall Navigations,* ed. 1589, is an account of the voyage of Captain Hore, which is brief but very interesting. I condense it as follows : In the year 1536 Master Hore, with two ships, the " Trinitie" and " Minion," set sail from Gravesend about the end of April. He had six score persons with him " whereof 30 were gentlemen." They reached Cape Breton in two months, and mention is made of the great number of birds, similarly to Cartier's account. They sow " stores of beares, both blacke and white." Coming to a fire made by the savages, they found " the side of a beare on a wooden spit left at the same by the savages that were fledde. There in the same place they founde a boote of leather, garnished on the otter side of the calfe with certaine brave trailes, as it were of raw silke, and also found a certaine great warm mitten." The query is, to whom the "boote" belonged. The account speaks of the famine they suffered, as their supplies gave out, and "they found small reliefe, more than that they had from the nest of an osprey, that brought hourly to her young great plentee of divers sorts of fishes." They had to subsist upon roots and herbs, but their famine increased and their hunger became such that "the fellowe killed his mate while hee stouped to take up a roote for his relief, and cutting out pieces of his body * * * * broyled the same on the coles and greedily devoured them." This continuing, "the company decreased," till the captain heard of the cannibalism, upon which he made a "notable oration," saying, among other things, that it was better to have perished in body, and to have everlasting life, than to have lived "for a poore time" and been doomed to the unquenchable fire of hell. He exhorted them to pray to God for relief. "And such was the mercie of God that the same night there arrived a French shippe in that port, well furnished with vittaile, and such was the policie of the English, that they became masters of the same, and, changing ships and vitailing them, they set sail to come into England." They reached St. Ives, in Cornwall, about the end of October.

*De Prato.*—Hakluyt's *Principall Navigations*, ed. 1589, page 517, has a short account entitled "The voiage of the two ships, whereof one was called the 'Dominus Vobiscum,' set out the 20th day of May, in the 29 yeere of King Henry the Eight, and in the yeere of Our Lord God 1527, for the discovery of the north partes." The following sentence occurs in the account : "And it hath been told mee by Sir Martin Frobisher and Master Richard Allen, a Knight of the Sepulchre, that a Canon of S. Paul in London, which was a great mathematician and a man indued with wealth, did much advaunce the action, and went therein himselfe in person, but what his name was, I cannot learne of any." This voyage was made under "Master Robert Thorne of Bristoll."

*The Bretons.*—Herrera (ed. 1728, dec. iii., l. x. cap. 9) says that in 1526 the Breton, Nicholas Don, pursued the fisheries at Baccalaos. Purchas in his *Pilgrimages* says that Rut reports that in 1527 eleven sail of Normans and one of Bretons were at St. John. Lescarbot says (*Nouvelle France*, 1612, page 22) that Baron de Léry landed cattle on the Isle of Sable in 1528. Ramusio (in *Raccolta*, 1556, iii., 424) says : "Li Brettoni & Normandi, per la qual causa è chiamata questa terra il capo delli Brettoni," *i. e.*, the Bretons and Normans, for which reason the land was named Cape Breton. The "discorso," from which the above is taken, is that of the *Gran Capitano Francese*, of 1539, held by some writers to be Jean Parmentier of Dieppe. This "discorso" states that the Bretons and Normans visited these coasts thirty-five years previously, that is in 1504; also that Jean Denys, of Honfleur, and the pilot Camarto (Gamort), of Rouen, sailed to this Cape Breton in 1506, and, in 1508, "un navilio di Dieppa detto la 'Pensee'" (a ship of Dieppe, the 'Pensee'), carried thither "Thomas Aubert."

Gosselin (*Documents authentiques et inédits*, etc., Rouen, 1876) says the following ships sailed to Newfoundland in 1508: "Bonne-Aventure," "Sibille," "Michel," and "Marie de Bonne Nouvelles." Mr. George Dexter, writing of this period in an article on "Cortereal, Verrazano, Gomez, Thevet," has the following concise paragraph: "The consolidation of France into one great kingdom may be said to date from 1524, when the death of Claude, the wife of Francis I., vested the hereditary right to the succession of Brittany in the crown of France. The marriage of Charles VIII. with Anne, Claude's mother, in 1491, had brought the last of the feudal chiefs into subjection, but it required many years to make the inhabitants of these provinces Frenchmen, and the rulers at Paris exercised little authority over the towns and principalities of the interior. The coasts of Normandy and Brittany were peopled by a race of adventurous mariners, some of them exercising considerable power, as, for instance, the Angos of Dieppe, one of whom (Jean) was ennobled and created Viscount and Captain of that town. Such places as Dieppe, Honfleur, St. Malo and others had already furnished men and leaders for voyages of exploration and discovery. These had made expeditions to the Canaries and the African coast and the fishing population of the French provinces were not unused to voyages of considerable length. They were not slow, then, in seeking a share in the advantages offered by the new countries discovered by Cabot and Cortereal, and they speedily became skilful and powerful in the American fisheries. The fishermen of the ports of Brittany are known to have reached the Newfoundland shores as early as 1504. They have left there an enduring trace in the name of Cape Breton, which, in one form or another, is found upon very early maps. Two years afterward Jean Denys, who was from Honfleur, is said to have visited the Gulf of St. Lawrence, and to have made a chart of it; but what now passes for such a chart is clearly of a later origin."

Thers is a copy of this map in the Parliament Library at Ottawa, but it is claimed that it is "absolument apocryphe," and a search in the French Archives discloses no original.

The "Jean Angos" mentioned by Mr. Dexter is thus spoken of by

10

Ramusio (*Raccolta* iii., 424, ed. 1556) : "Giovan Ango, Padre del Monsignor lo Capitano & Visconte di Dieppa."

*The Maps.*—The map of Canada, as given by Ramusio in his *Navigationi*, iii, 425, is stated to have been drawn by Gastaldi. The map of Hochelaga is at page 446, ed. 1556. The Cabot mappemonde (1544) contains the first recognition in a printed map of the Cartier voyages. The original is now in the possession of the French Government. Photographs of it are in several American libraries. It is said there were four editions of this map, "of which a single copy of one edition is now known." It was discovered in Germany, in 1843. It is described by D'Avezac in *Bulletin de la Societé de Geographie*, 4 ser. xiv. 268-70, 1857.

*To view a haven and small river.*—See Hawkins' *Picture of Quebec,* page 62, quoted by LeMoine in *Picturesque Quebec*, page 399, *et seq.* If, as is claimed, Roberval wintered here also, it is strange that no mention is made of the fort erected by Cartier. The claim that Cartier wintered here in 1541-42, is probably true, but that Roberval wintered here the following season (1543-44) admits of much doubt for reasons stated elsewhere.

*And certain Portugals.*—A thorough search in the Spanish and Portuguese archives may yet give more particulars of Cartier and his times.

*Isle of Ascension.*—This is Anticosti, called by the Indians then Natiscotec.

*Isle of Orleans.*—There is an historical *brochure* on this island written by Turcotte.

*Michael Gaillon was hanged.*—Probably the first case of hanging in Canada.

*Paint themselves for fear of heat, etc.*—It is said the Hottentots rubbed themselves with grease and oil for the same purpose.

*16th April, 1542.*—See life of Cartier at commencement of this book.

*France Roy.*—See preceding note.

*Over against Tartary, etc.*—The wish was father to the thought. All the early expeditions thought to reach the East Indies.

*Jaques Noël.*—Of him Lescarbot says (ed. 1612, page 418): "Thus, in the year 1588, Sieur de la launaye Chaton and Jaques Noël, nephews and heirs of the said Cartier, * * * * * * So that they were obliged to seek aid from the King, to whom they presented a petition to have a commission granted them similar to that which had formerly been given to their uncle Cartier, in consideration of his services, and that in the voyage of 1540, he had used the sum of 1638 livres more than he had received, which had never been returned to him. As King, in addition, also, for the purpose of forming a French colony, a monopoly (*privilege*) for twelve years of the trade with the savages in those lands, especially in furs, all the subjects of the King to be forbidden to engage in this trade, nor interfere in any way (for the twelve years) with them in the enjoyment of this privilege, and of several mines which they discovered. Letters patent and the commission were granted the 14th January, 1588." Owing, however, to the jealousy and machinations of the merchants of St. Malo, who, "as soon as they heard of the commission and the monopoly, straightway presented a petition to the Privy Council of the King to have it annulled. And their request was carried out the 5th May following."

*Cartier's Men* (second voyage.)—Jacques Cartier's officers and crew as in the archives of Saint Malo, France:—

Jacques Cartier, Capne.

Thomas Fourmont, Me. de la nef.

Guille, Le Breton Bastille, capne. et pilote du Galion.

Jacq. Maingar me du Galion.

Marc Jalobert, capne. et pilote du Courlien.

Guille de Marié, me de Courlien.

Laurent Boulain.

Estienne Nouel

Pierre Esmery dect Talbot.

Michel Herné.

Estienne Reumevel.

Michel Audiepore.

Bertrande Samboste.

Richard Lebay, Faucamps.

Lucas Pere Sr. ou Lucas Jacq. Sr. Fammys.

Francois Guiteault, apotecaire.

Georges Mabille.

Guillme Lequart, charpentier.

Robin Le Fort.

Samson Ripault, barbier.

Françoys Guillot.

Guille Esnault, charpentier.

Jehan Dabin, charpentier.

Jehan Duvert

Eustache Grossin.

Guillme Allierte.

Jehan Ravy.

Pierres Marquier, trompet.

Guille Legentilhomme.

Raoullet Maingard.

Francois Duault.

Herné Henry.

Yvon Legal.

Antoine Alierte.

Jehan Colas.

Jacq. Pouisault.

Dom Guille Le Breton.

Dom Antoine.

Phillipe Thomas, charpentier.

Jacq. Duboys.

Julien Planternet.

Jehan Go.

Jehan Legentilhomme.

Michel Douquais, charpentier.

Jehan Aismery, charpentier.

Pierre Maugart.

Lucas Clauier.

Gaulset Rion.

Jehan Jacq. de Morbihan.

Pierre Nyel.

Legendre Estienne Leblanc.

Julien Golet.
Thomas Boulain.
Michel Philipot.
Jehan Hamel.
Jehan Fleury.
Guille Guilbert.
Colas Barbe.
Laurens Gaillot.
Guille Bochier.
Jehan Margen.
Geoffrey Ollivier.
Guille de Guerneze.

Jehan Pierres.
Jehan Commuyres.
Anthoine Desgrauches.
Louys Donayrer.
Pierre Conpeaulx.
Pierres Jonchée.
Michel Eon.
Jean Anthoine.
Michel Maingard.
Bertrand Apurie.
Giles Staffin.

These are the names given in the *liste d'equipage* preserved at Saint Malo. The following additional names should be added:—

Jean Gouyon.
Charles Gaillot.
Jean Poullet.
De Goyelle.

Claude de Pontbrians.
Charles de la Pommeraye.
Philippe Rougemont.

*Labrador.*—This name was given to this district, according to a paper in the Transactions of the Quebec L. and H. Society for 1843, as a Basque whaler of this name visited the coast in the latter part of the 15th century. Sir William Dawson says the Breton sailor here stood in the presence of the equivalent of the flint folk of his own country.

*Jacques Quartier, the Pilot.*— " Gerald, eleventh Earl of Kildare was born on the 26th February, 1525. He was ten years of age at the time of his brother's arrest, and then lying ill with the small-pox at Donore, in the County Kildare. He was committed to the care of his tutor, Thomas Leverons, who conveyed him in a large basket into Offaly to his sister, Lady Mary O'Connor. There he remained until he was perfectly recovered. The misfortunes of his family had excited great sympathy for the boy over the whole of Ireland. This made the Government anxious to have him in their power, and they endeavored accordingly to induce O'Brien to surrender him to them. About the 5th March, 1540, Lady Eleanor O'Donnel, suspecting that it was the intention of her husband to surrender Gerald to the English Government, resolved to send him away. She engaged a merchant vessel of St. Malo, which happened to be in Donegal Bay, to convey a small party to the coast of Brittany. Bartholomew Warner, an agent of the English Government, sends the following account of this transaction to Sir John Wallop, the English ambassador in France :—" After ther departing from Yrlande they arryved at Murles (Morlaix) wher, as he was well recyvyd of the captayne, whiche leadde him throughe the towne by the hande, wher he tarryed 3 or 4 days and strayght-wayes the captayne sent word to Monsieur de Chattebriande off ther arrivying ther.  *  *  *  *   And from thens they came in the sayde shippe to Saynt Malo, wher he was also well receyvyd of them of the town, and specially of Jacques Quartier, the pilot, which your Lordship spoke off at my being at Rouene." *The Earls of Kildare and their Ancestors, from* 1057 *to* 1773, by the Marquis of Kildare ; 3rd edition, pp. 179, 196.  Cartier was called " el corsario Jacques Cartier" by the Spanish ambassador in France, making a report of Cartier and Roberval's expedition.  (Navarrette *Bibliotheca maritima,* vol. i., page 396.

Mr. J. M. LeMoine, in " Picturesque Quebec," 1882, page 428, thus writes of Ringfield, a country seat in the environs of Quebec : "Close to the Dorchester Bridge to the west, on the Charlesburg road, there was once an extensive estate known as Smithville. *  *  *  *   Some hundred acres, comprising the land on the west of the ruisseau Lairet, known as *Ferme des Anges,* were detached from it and now form Ringfield.  *  *  *  *   In rear it is bounded to the west by the little stream called Lairet, with the ruisseau St. Michel in view ; to the south its boundary is the meandering Cahire Coubat.  (Cahire Coubat, expressive of windings according to Lagard, called by Jacques Cartier the River Ste. Croix, and afterwards denominated the River St. Charles in compliment, says La Potherie, to Charles de Boues, Grand Vicar of Pontoise, founder of the first mission of the Recollets in New France.)  *  *  *  *  *   The precise spot in the St. Charles where Cartier moored his vessels, and where his people built the fort in which they wintered, may have been, for aught that could be advanced to the contrary, where the French Government in 1759 built the hornwork or earth redoubt, so plainly visible to this day near the Lairet stream.  It may also have been at the mouth of the St. Michel stream which here empties itself into the St. Charles, on the Jesuits' farm.  *  *  *  *  *   Jacques Cartier's fort, we know to a certainty, must have been on the north bank of the river.  *  *  *  *  *   (Writers seem to agree that Cartier wintered in the St. Charles on the Jesuits' property."

" The exact spot in the River St. Charles where Cartier moored his vessel, is supposed, on good authority, to have been the site of the old bridge (a little higher up than the present) called Dorchester Bridge, where there is a ford at low water, close to the Marine Hospital.  That it was on the east bank, not far from the former residence of Chas. Smith, Esq., is evident from the river having been frequently crossed by the natives coming from Stadacona to visit their " French guests." (Hawkins' *Picture of Quebec*, p. 47.)

*The River St. Charles.*—The river St. Charles, according to La Potherie, was named after Charles des Boües, Grand Vicar of Pontoise, the founder of the first mission of Recollets in New France.

*Le Canon de Bronze.*—The contention that Cartier wintered at the river now called the Jacques Cartier has long since been shown to be utterly erroneous. " Le canon de bronze," an article published in the second volume of the Transactions of the Literary and Historical Society of Quebec, endeavors to explain the Indian pantomime to prevent Cartier visiting Hochelaga as a warning of the assumed fate of Verazzano. (See note, "Where Cartier wintered.")

*The Remains of the " Petite Hermine."*—The city surveyor of Quebec, Mr. Jas. Hamel, called the attention of the Literary and Historical Society of Quebec to the remains of a vessel lying at the brook St. Michel, supposed to be the " Petite Hermine."

*Le Canadien*, of August 25th, 1843, has the following: "At the invitation of Mr. Jos. Hamel, city surveyor, Hon. Wm. Sheppard, the president, and Mr. Faribault, vice-president, of the Literary and Historical Society of Quebec, went with him on Saturday, the 19th inst., to visit the place, and according to the position of the *debris* of the vessel, the nature of the wood it is composed of, and the character of the stones (ballast) found at the bottom, they were satisfied that all the probabilities are in favor of Mr. Hamel's hypothesis. On a report of this visit, the Council of the Literary and Historical Society assembled on Monday last and resolved on laying open the *debris*, leaving it to Mr. Faribault, the vice-president, to make, with Mr. Hamel, the necessary arrangements for the execution of this work. The members of the Council having no funds at their disposal that they can legally apply to this purpose, have so far carried it on at their own expense. Some valuable evidences of the ancient existence of this vessel have been gathered. We shall give them in giving an account of the exhumation in progress under the direction of Messrs. Faribault and Hamel. All those who can throw any light on the subject, either of their own knowledge or by what they may have learned by tradition, are earnestly solicited to impart the same at the office of *Le Canadien*. These gentlemen ought not to be allowed to carry on this work at their sole expense. The country, the world, are interested in it. This continent in 1535, from end to end one vast wilderness, the imagination can scarcely figure to itself a more awful solitude than that in which, during the winter of 1535-1536, Cartier and his faithful followers, amidst savages in an unknown country, buried in the dreary swamp (for it then must have been little better) of Sainte Croix, now the beautifnl valley of the St. Charles, covered with cheerful cottages and a redundant population. * * * * * * * During the dismal winter, Jacques Cartier must have passed in his new quarters at Ste. Croix, he lost, by sickness contracted, it is said, from the natives, but more probably from scurvy, twenty-five of his men. This obliged him to abandon one of his three vessels (La Petite Hermine, it is believed), which he left in her winter quarters, returning with the two others to France. The *locale* of the *debris* or remains not only correspond with the description given by Jacques Cartier of Ste. Croix, but also with the attention and particular care that might be expected from a skilful commander, in the selection of a safe spot in an unknown region, where never a European had been before him, for wintering his vessels. They lie in the bottom of a small creek or gulley known as the ruisseau St. Michel, into which the tides regularly flow, on the property of Charles Smith, Esq., on the north side of the St. Charles, and at about half a mile following the bends of the river above the site of the old Dorchester Bridge. They are a little up the creek at about an acre from its mouth, and their position (where a sudden or short turn of the creek renders it next to impossible that she should be forced out of it by any rush of water in the spring or efforts of the ice) evinces at once the precaution and the judgment of the commander in his choice of the spot. But small portions of her remaining timber are visible through the mud, but they are bitumenized and black as ebony, and after reposing in that spot 307 years seem, as far as, by chopping them with axes or spades and probing by iron rods or picks, can be ascertained, sound as the day they were brought thither. The merit of the discovery belongs to our fellow-townsman, Mr. Joseph Hamel, the city surveyor."

The Quebec *Gazette* of August 30th, 1843, speaks of the above article as follows :—" In the last number of *Le Canadien*, there is an article of deep interest to the Canadian antiquarian. The long agitated question as to the *where* or *whereabouts* Jacques Cartier, on his second voyage from France to this continent, spent the winter of 1535–1536, whether at the embouchure of the river bearing his name, emptying into the St. Lawrence some ten or eleven leagues above Quebec, or in the little river St. Charles to the north of and at the foot of the promontory on which Quebec is built, is now, it would seem, about to be solved and satisfactorily set at rest by the recent discovery of the remains of a vessel, doubtless of European construction, supposed to be those of 'La Petite Hermine,' of about sixty tons burthen, one of the three ('La Grande Hermine,' 'La Petite Hermine' and 'L'Emerillon') with which, on the 19th May, 1535, that intrepid navigator left St. Malo."

A certain portion of these relics were sent to the museum at St. Malo, and are described by Dr. N. E. Dionne, Quebec, as follows:— "It is in the museum that the most interesting souvenir of Jacques Cartier is to be found. It is well known that during his second voyage to Canada, Cartier was forced to abandon one of his vessels, 'La Petite Hermine,' in the River St. Charles, at the mouth of the brook Lairet. Three hundred years later remains of this vessel were found, which were divided into two portions. One portion remained at Quebec, and was burned in the Parliament fire, and the other was sent to St. Malo. A trophy in the form of a pyramid was made of them. At the apex was placed pulley blocks and bolts; beneath are the remains of the ship knees and ribs. The body of the pyramid is made up of pieces of the timbers and irons. the following inscription has been placed on the largest piece: 'À LA MÉMOIRE DE JACQUES CARTIER ET DES BRAVES MARINS, SES COMPAGNONS,' and below this, ' *Débris du navire 'La Petite Hermine,' de St. Malo, que Jacques Cartier fut contraint d'abandonner au Canada en avril, 1536.*' * * * * * * These remains of 'La Petite Hermine' were covered with five feet of mud when discovered after 300 years."

In the same museum is a portrait of Cartier, painted by Riss, which is about seven feet by five, and is probably the original of the prints known in Canada. (See Transactions 1862, Que. Lit. & His. Soc.).

Mr. J. M. Le Moine writes : * * * * 'The gentleman in our Literary and Historical Society, G. B. Faribault, who had given much time to the study of Cartier's Voyages, left this world, I regret to say, * * * many years ago. Under his superintendence, our Society published, in 1843, a version of Jacques Cartier's voyages, with notes and plates, Ramusio's, I think. * * * * * The remains of 'Petite Hermine,' deposited in our museum by my old friends, Faribault and Hamel, were destroyed by fire in 1849, I think. * * * * * * It was Mr. Hovens who was Mayor of St. Malo when the late Theophile Hamel, the artist, procured the portrait we now have of Jacques Cartier; the original in oil, made by Hamel, is at the Laval, I think."

* * * * * * * * *

A letter was received by the writer from the Rev. Thomas E. Hamel, Bibliothecain of Laval University, in answer to several queries at the time that the interesting and valuable collection of portraits, etc., was being shown in the Natural History Rooms, Montreal, under the auspices of the Montreal Numismatic and Antiquarian Society. The reverend gentleman states that the painting of the Elevation of the Cross, *fleurdelysée*, by Cartier on the banks of the St. Charles, was painted by a Canadian artist, Mr. Hawksett; at least it was done by him at Quebec, "under the inspiration of our illustrious antiquarian, Mr. Faribault, whose property it was, and who deeded it to Laval University. Mr. Hawksett visited the locality to catch the spirit of the scene." The reverend gentleman closes his kind letter with a few lines regretting his lack of time to devote himself more fully to the study of early Canadian history, in which he is very deeply interested, and which, by his talents he would certainly be able to throw some light upon in an interesting manner.

In the catalogue of the "loan exhibition" referred to above the painting of the Elevation of the Cross is attributed to Hamel.

*Savages from New France.*—At page 23, vol. vii., of the publications of the Hakluyt Society, is to be read : "A note of Sebastian Gabote's voyage, taken out of an old chronicle, written by Robert Fabian, some time alderman of London, which is in the custodie of John Stowe, citizen, etc." Then follows the "note," from which I make the following excerpt: "This yeere (in 1498) also were brought unto the King, three men taken in the new founde Iland, that before I spake of in William Purchas time, being Maior. These were clothed in beastes skinnes and ate rawe fleshe and spake such speech that no man coulde understande them, and in their demeanour like to brute beastes, whom the King kept a time after. Of the which upon two yeares past (1501) after I saw two apparelled after the manner of Englishmen, in Westminster pallace, which at that time I coulde not discerne from Englishemen till I was learned what they were. But as for speeche, I heard none of them utter one worde." This extract is reprinted from Hakluyt's *Divers Voyages*, 1582. It also occurs in his *Principall Navigations*, 1589, page 515. Before meeting with this passage I had the following line in my note book: "Savages brought from the Newfoundland were shown in England in 1502. (Purchas' Pilgrimages, page 915, ed, 1617.) In 1508 savages were brought to France by Captain Thomas Aubert, of Dieppe. *Relation de la Nouvelle France*, par le P. Biard, 1616. In the *Eusebii Chronicon*, Paris, 1512, is an account of the visit of American savages to Rouen in 1509. There is a bas-relief over a tomb in the church of St. Jacques, of Dieppe, in which American natives are represented (Margry's *Les Navigations Françaises*, appendix ii., 371 *et seq*). Cortereal's expedition brought savages to Lisbon on 11th October, 1501.

## 154

*Sieur de Roberval.*—At page 410 of Lescarbot, edition 1612, is the following :—"After the discovery of the Grand River of Canada, made by Captain Quartier, in the manner we have related, the King in the year 1540 appointed as his Lieutenant-General in the new lands of Canada, Hochelaga and Saguenay and surrounding countries, Jean François de la Roque, Sieur de Roberval, a nobleman of Vimen in Picardy, to whom he caused to be delivered his commission the 15th January, the same year, to the effect that he should go and dwell in those lands, build forts there, and take settlers there. And in order that this might be done, His Majesty had given to him forty-five thousand livres by Jean Du Val, his treasurer. Jacques Quartier was named by His Majesty the Captain-General and Master Pilot over all the vessels to be engaged in the enterprise, numbering five, and of a tonnage of four hundred tons, as I find in the accounts of the monies rendered by the said Quartier, which were communicated to me by Sieur Samuel Georges Bourgeois de la Rochelle. Now, not having been able up to the present to see (*recouvrer*) Roberval's commission (this may be found in the Actes de Belleval, notaire à Bourdeaux, 3rd avril, 1541, quoted in part by Faillon, in *Histoire de la Colonie Française*, tome 1, p. 40; see note 'Roberval's Commission'), I will satisfy myself with giving my readers that which shortly afterwards was given to Cartier, of which the following is the import: ' Francis, by the grace of God, King of France, to all to whom these presents may come; greeting: With the desire of having a wider and fuller knowledge of the several countries said to be inhabited and in the possession of savage peoples, living without a knowledge of God, we have had, at much expense, several enterprises, under good pilots and under experienced and learned subjects, who have brought among us several savages, who have been for a long time in our kingdom, instructing them in the love and fear of God, of his St. Louis and Christian belief, with the intention of taking them back to those countries with quite a number of our own subjects willing to go, in order the more easily to lead other savages to a belief in our Holy Faith ; and, among others, we have sent our dear and well-beloved Jacques Cartier, who has discovered the large countries of Canada and Hochelaga, making a part of Asia on the West ; which countries he has found (so he has reported to us) rich in several articles, the people healthy and well-formed, and well disposed, of whom he brought back a certain number whom we have had instructed in our Holy Faith. In consideration of which and of their good inclinations, we have determined to send Quartier back to Canada and Hochelaga as far as Saguenay (if he can reach there), with a good number of ships and various articles of manufacture, etc., that he may make further discoveries, study the peoples more, and dwell with them (if necessary) in order to the better carrying out our plan and please God our Creator and Redeemer, in honor of His Holy name, and of our Holy Mother Catholic Church, of which we are called and named the first son. And as it is necessary for the better ordering and celerity of the said enterprise to appoint and name a Captain-General and Master-Pilot to be in charge of the ships and men, be it known that having full confidence in the said Jacques Cartier, in his loyalty, experience, endurance and other good qualities, we have appointed, ordered and established him, and do hereby appoint, order and establish him by these presents Captain-General and Master-Pilot of all the ships and other vessels we order to take part in this expedition, and he is to hold, have and enjoy these prerogatives, etc., so long as it may please us. And we have given, and do give him, authority to appoint to the ships such lieutenants and other officers as may be necessary, and as many as he may require for the expedition. And we give orders to our Admiral or Vice-Admiral that the said Jacques Quartier be recognized as Captain-General and Master-Pilot, with all the prerogatives, rights, etc. In addition to which he is permitted to take the small gallion, named " L'Emerillon," which he now has from us, which is now old, to serve to put in repair those vessels of which he has need, and of which he need not render us any account ; of which account we relieve him by these presents. By these also we command our provosts of Paris, bailiffs of Rouen, Caen, Orleans, Blois, Tours, our seneschals of Maine, Anjou, Guiene, and to all our other bailiffs, seneschals, provosts and officers of justice, both of our kingdom and of Brittany, in charge of any prisoners accused or convicted of any crimes except treason, or uttering false money, to give them over to the said Quartier, his clerks or deputies, for service in this expedition, such prisoners as are judged suitable, to the number of fifty, whom Quartier may choose ; to be chosen from those judged and sentenced for their crimes ; and if from those accused in civil matters, those interested to be satisfied ; we do not wish Quartier to be delayed in his work, however. Satisfaction is to be levied on their goods only. And the said giving up of the prisoners to Quartier, we wish to be done, for the purpose above mentioned, by our officers of justice in spite of any opposition, however made, and in the manner aforesaid. And in order that no more than fifty be taken, we wish that the delivery of each one made to Quartier be entered and written on the margin of these presents, and that particulars in writing be sent to our beloved Chancellor, so as to know the number and quality of those given over. For such is our pleasure. In witness of which we have caused to be attached hereto our seal. Given at Saint Pris the seventeenth day of October, 1540, and of our reign the twenty-sixth. Also signed on the fold: By the King, His Chancellor, and others. De la Chesnaye. And sealed on the fold and sealed with a drop of yellow wax. Matters having thus been arranged, De Roberval and Quartier set sail for the New Lands, and intrenched themselves (*se fortifierent*) at Cape Breton, where are still to be seen remains of their habitation. But relying too much on the generosity of the King, without seeking the means of subsistence in the country itself; and the King being occupied with weighty matters pressing upon France at that time, had not any way of sending a new stock of provisions to those who should have got their subsistence in the country, after having had such a generous start from His Majesty, and Roberval having been sent out to serve the King, as I find in the account given by Quartier, that he took eight months to go and get him after he had remained there seventeen months. And I must think that the *habitation* of Cape Breton was not less disastrous (*funeste*) than was that of St. Croix, made six years previously on the Grand River of Canada, where Quartier wintered. For this country being situated on the border of the lands and on the Gulf of Canada, which is always full of ice till the end of May, there is no doubt it is very cold and severe, and under an inclement sky. So that the failure of this expedition was due to the severity of the climate. And this could easily have been avoided, as the country is so large that a place might have been selected more to the south than to the north."

*Cartier Himself.*—André Thevet, a native of Argentine, states in his *Singularités de la France Antarctique,* published in 1558, that Cartier himself related to him the particulars of the first voyage and of the one made the following year.

*Where Cartier wintered during the Second Voyage.*—Champlain, in his early voyages, visited the small river fifteen leagues above Quebec, which he thought to be the site of Achelay, spoken of by Cartier; this river had been called by some the St. Croix, and thus it had been commonly concluded that here was where Cartier had wintered. Hence the river was named the Jacques Cartier, which name it bears to this day. Champlain, in the 1613 edition, page 191, demonstrates the falsity of this being the place where Cartier had wintered. This was overlooked by Le Clercq, Charlevoix and others, and the error perpetuated till a later day. Champlain says in the 1640 edition, page 10, that the river which Cartier named

St. Croix was then called St. Charles. Champlain states further that the ruins of a chimney were to be seen, pieces of square timber and several cannon balls. Sagard, Lescarbot and de la Potherie confirm Champlain's statement that Cartier wintered on the St. Charles. On Lescarbot's map, ed. 1612, Stadaconé and Saint Croix are placed together at some distance above Quebec, which is of course an error.

Faillon believes that Cartier ascended as far as the Lachine Rapids on his first visit to Hochelaga.

*The Epidemic.*—Charlevoix states that Hochelaga had three palisades surrounding it. He was evidently mistaken, as the map in Ramusio proves. Charlevoix also says that the epidemic among Cartier's followers was due to their cohabiting with the savages; that the savages had never suffered from it, and that Cartier had been sick with the disease. The only account we have of the epidemic is that left in the second voyage of Cartier, so that these assertions of Charlevoix are mere assumptions. Another false statement made by Charlevoix is that one of Cartier's ships was lost by shipwreck during the second voyage; this is disproved again by Cartier's statement that he had to leave one vessel behind and set sail in the other two, owing to loss of men through the epidemic. Probably the story is to be accounted for by the fact that Roberval some years later lost a barque, with its crew of eight, in the St. Lawrence, having left Charlebourg with eight barques and a crew of eight to explore "Saguenay."

*Were Priests With Cartier ?*—The Revd. B. F. DaCosta, D.D., in an article on Cartier in the "Narrative History of America," edited by Justin Winsor, doubts that Cartier had priests with him, while by others it is maintained that Cartier had priests with him, and for the following reasons:—Francis I., the King of France, wished to spread the Roman Catholic religion; and that they accompanied Cartier seems to be proved by the following expressions:—*Aprés avoir ouï la messe.*  *  *  *  *  *  *Le dimanche nous fîmes dire la messe.* And during the epidemic, mass was celebrated before an image of the Virgin Mary placed against a tree ; *la messe dit et chantée devant la dite image.* And in the fourth chapter of the second voyage Cartier distinctly says " the priests " had spoken to Jesus. In the list of Cartier's officers and crew (to be found on another page) are two names, Dom Guille. le Breton and Dom Antoine ; of these Faillon says in his *Histoire de la Colonie Francaise,* 1st vol., page 510, that they were undoubtedly priests, probably of the order of St. Benoit, of which order all the priests had the prefix "Dom." The first time mass was said in Canada, according to the second chapter of the second voyage, was on the 7th September, 1535. Mention is made in the second voyage of a request by the savages to be baptized. Cartier replied to this that he would bring priests with him on another voyage. Faillon takes this to mean that the priests with him were ignorant of the Indian language and could not therefore give the necessary instruction preceding the rite. During the epidemic, related in the 15th chapter of the second voyage, mention is made of the placing of a statue of the Virgin Mary on a tree outside the fort, and of the celebration of high mass and of a procession to the statue. This is certainly the first religious procession in Canada. In the archives of St. Malo (1538) is a record of the baptism of three savages brought there by Cartier (*Massachusetts Archives, Documents Collected in France*, 1, p. 367.)

*La Nouvelle France.*—In the map to be found in the third volume of Ramusio edition, 1556, page 424, are to be seen the words "La Nuova Francia." Faillon states that Cartier himself gave the name of "New France." *Histoire de la Colonie Francaise*, vol. 1, page 512. In the *Commerce de l'Amerique*, tome 1, page 9, is the following:— "Nous avons même la carte de differents côtes propres à faire la pêche de la morue, publiée en 1506." Charlevoix, in his "Fastes Chronologiques," mentions one published in 1506 by Jean Denis de Honfleur. Whether the term "New France" is in it, the writer does not know.

*Did Cartier Write the Accounts of the Voyages?*—Faillon reasons, concerning the manuscript which he consulted in the Bibliothèque Impériale, that it was written by Cartier himself, and that he also wrote the accounts of the first and third voyages (of which, however, no manuscripts are known, though there are three of the second voyage). In the account the third person is used, but in the dedication the first person is used. In the account of the third voyage occurs :—" *Le roi ayant ouï ce qu'avait rapporté le Capitaine Cartier de ses deux premiers voyages tant par ses ecrits que verbalement.*" Here is a distinct statement that the King read Cartier's accounts and conversed with him concerning his two voyages. Jacques Noël, his nephew and heir, in a letter in 1587, attributes to him expressly the authorship of the voyages :—" *Je ne manquerai pas de m'informer par moi-même, s'il y a moyen de trouver ces relations, que le Capitaine Jacques Cartier a écrites après ses deux derniers voyages en Canada.*" Mr. J. Winter Jones, of the British Museum, in vol. vii. of the publications of the Hakluyt Society, says it does not appear that any of these journals were written by Cartier ; in fact, the presumption is the other way. He gives no reasons.

*The Hurons.*—The Indians Cartier came in contact with at Quebec were doubtless Huron-Iroquois. An elaborate note by Faillon in the first volume of *Histoire de la Colonie Francaise,* goes to prove this, and to overthrow the argument of Sir William Dawson that they were Algonquins.

*Limoilou.*—Limoilou is thus described by Dr. N. E. Dionne in a valuable paper on Cartier published in the *Courrier du Canada* 24th September, 1885 : "Limoilou is distant seven or eight miles from St. Malo. The residence of Jacques Cartier is quite large and in good preservation. In the tower to the right is a winding staircase giving access to each floor. The *salon* is on the first, and contains a superb fireplace of beautifully carved stone. On the wall is to be seen the coat of arms of the former master of the house (*maître de céans*) supported by two kneeling female figures. This has been injured considerably. The hand of the vandals of '93 has been here."

A piece of the window from Limoilou was brought to Montreal several years ago and is in the possession of L'Union Allet of Montreal. It certainly does not date back to the time of Cartier.

*The 350th Anniversary.*—On the evening of the 23rd September, 1885, at Quebec, the Cercle Catholique celebrated the 350th anniversary of the arrival of Cartier at Quebec, which took place on the 14th September, 1535. Our system of dating having been changed in 1582, it was held that the anniversary of the arrival is really the 24th September. The celebration was a great success, whether or not the 14th or 24th be held as the proper anniversary.

*The Savages.*—Elaborate notes have been given by numerous writers on the savages at the time of Cartier's visit, as to what tribes they belonged, etc. A volume would be necessary to discuss the question fully and intelligently, and it is to be hoped that some writer will take up the subject. As to their language, it is certain that those living in the districts about the fisheries had learned some Basque words from their intercourse with the Basques, such as *bacaillos* for codfish (their own word was *apege*), which had begun years before Cartier's visit. In Verazzano's short account, to be found in the third volume of Ramusio, page 420, ed. 1556, the statement occurs that the savages were very susceptible to religious instruction. This was written at Dieppe on the 8th July, 1524. In Cartier's first voyage the trading of furs and the making of the sign of the cross with his fingers by one of the savages proved they had had intercourse with Europeans. An interesting note is given by Père Lalemant a century later ; he wrote from Quebec in 1626 :— " Les sauvages de ce pays appellent le soleil *Jésus* et l'on tient ici que les Basques qui y ont ci-devant habité, sont les auteurs de ce denomination " (*Relation de la Nouvelle France, annèe* 1626, *p.* 4). Read Montaigne's essay " On Cannibals."

*The Site of Hochelaga.*—In an article contributed by the writer to the Montreal *Gazette* the latter portion reads as follows:—" Now, to consider where Cartier landed and where Hochelaga was situated. In the narrative it is stated that the town is near a mouatain which is around it ; that the town was distant two leagues from the place where Cartier went ashore ; that the town was distant a quarter of a league from the mountain, and then is related what can be seen from the summit, as " in the middle of the plain we could see the river further up than our boats were, etc." It would appear from this that Cartier landed somewhere opposite Nun's Island, and the site of the town was either near the present village of Côte des Neiges or near Peel and Sherbrooke streets. The Côte des Neiges theory accords best with the statement surrounded by a mountain But in favor of the Peel street site is that it is about a quarter of a league from the mountain and that Indian relics have been found there; these are in the Natural History Society's collection, and are described by Sir J. W. Dawson in the *Canadian Naturalist*, vol. v., page 430, and vol. vi., page 362. He is of the opinion that this was the ancient site of Hochelaga. The writer in 1868 and 1869 found pieces of Indian pottery in the same locality, that is, in the plot of land opposite the Prince of Wales terrace, which plot was at that time a vacant field.

*Francis I.*—Francis I., Count d'Angoulême, ascended the throne of France on the first of January, 1515, being then twenty-one years of age. His reign is one of the most interesting chapters in the history of France.

*Roberval's Commission.*—The first letters patent given Roberval were issued at Fontainebleau in the beginning of the year 1540 and created Roberval " lieutenant-general dans les terres neuves du Canada, etc.," with instructions to settle French families there and erect forts. On the 7th February, 1540, new letters patent were issued, registered at the Parliament of Paris on the 26th, authorizing him to take from certain prisons criminals condemned to death who might be thought suitable for the expedition, providing they were not guilty of high treason or counterfeiting. It was a condition that these men should maintain and support themselves during the two first years and should defray their own passages to New France. It was thought these prisoners would change from their evil ways. The King was anxious to teach the Indians religion, as the following excerpt from the commission shows :—" For the spreading of our holy Christian faith and for the advantage of our holy mother church and other good and just reasons, we have appointed François de la Roque, sieur de Roberval, our lieutenant-general and leader of forces in Canada and other countries not in the possession of any Christian prince. As, in waiting to have the number of men and volunteers necessary to people that country, the voyage cannot be undertaken as soon as we desire, and as the peoples (*créatures humaines*) live there without laws and without a knowledge of God and the holy Catholic faith, which we greatly desire to glorify and extend ; and as if this design were not carried out we would deeply regret it ; and as we have planned this to the glory of God our Creator, and anxious to please Him with all our heart, if it be His pleasure that the voyage have a successful termination ; for all these reasons and desiring to exercise mercy towards certain prisoners and evil-doers, so that they may know God, render thanks to Him and lead new lives, we order our officers of justice to deliver the number of criminals our lieutenant or his agents (*commis*) may select to take to those countries." (*Actes de Belleval*, notaire à Bordeaux, 3 Avril, 1541, quoted by Faillon.)

Francis I. gave ships three times to Verazzano, four times to Cartier and once to Roberval; in all about eighteen ships for expeditions to the New World.

*The Return of Cartier from the Third Voyage.*—Roberval and Cartier are asserted by Hakluyt to have met at the harbor of St. John, and that Cartier set sail the following night *secretly*. It is claimed that this is not correct. Champlain states that Roberval made Cartier return to the Island of Orleans where they made a settlement (*Voyages*, part ii., page 290, ed. 1632). Lescarbot says Roberval and Cartier made a settlement in Cape Breton (see note " Sieur de Roberval "). Roberval's own account states emphatically Cartier did not remain. Hakluyt says Roberval left Rochelle April 14th, 1542, reaching St. John on June 8th, and meeting Cartier here. DaCosta says in *Narrative and Critical History of America*, page 58, that Roberval must have been at this time in Canada, he having left Honfleur August 22, 1541, and not Rochelle on April 14th, 1542, as stated by Hakluyt. The ships met by Roberval at Newfoundland may have been those two despatched by Cartier to France under Jalobert and Noel during the previous autumn, or else Cartier on his way home met Sainterre. Thus Da Costa. It is hardly probable the ships of Jalobert and Noel were met. Faillon, in his *Histoire de la Colonie Francaise*, says that Cartier and Roberval met on the 8th June, 1542, at the harbor of St. John, and that Cartier left secretly the following night. Faillon states further that Roberval had left France 16th April, 1542, *Da Costa* making the

11

date of his departure about eight months earlier. It is possible Roberval may have wintered on the Atlantic coast and thus met Cartier in the spring. What were Cartier's motives is now a matter for mere surmise. It was fortunate, according to the experience of Roberval, that Cartier did not remain.

*The Expedition of* 1541.—The Spaniards thought to interfere in this, as Pope Alexander VI., by his famous bull, gave all America to Spain. The latter was not in a position then to maintain this right. (See Hazard's His. Collections I., 3-6 ; Chalmer's Political Annals, 10 ; Herrera I., 2-10 ; Irving's Columbus I., 185-200 ; Prescott's Ferdinand and Isabella II., 116, 174, 181 ; Thorne in Hakluyt's Divers Voyages).

*Jean Allefonsce, the Pilot of Roberval.*—" He was born at Saintonge, a village of Cognac. * * * Was mortally wounded in a naval combat near the Harbor of Rochelle, having followed the sea during a period of forty-one years. He appears to have been engaged in two special explorations. * * * Of the first —that connected with the Saguenay or vicinity, we have no account in the narrative which covers the voyage of Roberval." Father Leclercq says :—" The Sire Roberval writes that he undertook some considerable voyages to the Saguenay and several other rivers, etc." (*Premier établissement de la foy dans la Nouvelle France, Paris,* 1691). His *Cosmographie* in *MS.* is in the Bibliotheque Nationale, Paris. A copy of a portion of it was made for the Revd. B. F. Da Costa, D.D.

*Baccallaos.*—This word first occurs in Peter Martyr, 1516, as applied to the codfish.

*Dates of the Third Voyage.*—Da Costa epitomizes the third voyage as follows, and the writer has verified the authorities in nearly every case :—

Jan. 15, 1540—Roberval appointed Lieutenant-Governor [Harrisse, *Notes, etc.,* 243 to 253].

Feby. 6, 1540—Roberval took the oath [Harrisse, *Notes, etc.,* 243 to 253].

Feby. 7, 1540—Roberval receives the letters patent [Harrisse, *Notes, etc.,* 259 to 264].

Feby. 27, 1540—Roberval appoints Paul d'Angelhou (Sainterre) his lieutenant [Harrisse, *Notes, etc.,* 254 to 258].

March 9, 1540—Roberval authorized by Parliament of Rouen to take criminals [Harrisse, *Notes, etc.,* 268 to 271].

October 17, 1540—Cartier made master pilot and captain-general [*Quebec L. and H. Soc. Trans.,* 1862, p. 116].

October 28, 1540—Cartier receives letters patent from the Dauphin [*Quebec L. and H. Soc. Trans.*, 1862, p. 120].

Nov. 3, 1540—Fifty additional criminals ordered for the expedition [Gosselin's *Nouvelles Glanes Historiques Normandes*, Rouen, 1873, p. 4.

Decr. 12, 1540—King complains of delay [Harrisse, *J. and S. Cabot*, p. 212].

May 23, 1541—Cartier sails with five ships [Hakluyt iii., 232].

July 10, 1541—Chancellor Paget tells Rouen Parliament King complains of Roberval's delay [Gosselin's *Nouvelles Glanes*, p. 6].

Augt. 18, 1541—Roberval writes from Honfleur he will leave in four days [Gosselin's *Novelles Glanes*, p. 6].

Augt. 22, 1541—Roberval sailed from Honfleur [Gosselin's *Nouvelles Glanes*, p. 6].

Autumn, 1541—Roberval meets Jalobert and Noel at St. Johns [ditto and Hakluyt iii., 240].

Autumn, 1541—Roberval sends Sainterre to France [Hakluyt iii. 240].

Jany 26, 1542—Francis I. sends Sainterre back with supplies [Harrisse, *Notes*, p. 272].

Summer, 1542—Roberval builds France Roy [*Cosmographie* of Allefonsce ; Hakluyt iii., 241].

Sept. 9, 1542—Roberval pardons Sainterre for mutiny [Hakluy iii., 241].

Oct. 21, 1542—Cartier is at St. Malo [Quebec L. and H. S. *Transactions*, 1862, p. 93].

1542-1543—Roberval winters at France Roy [Hakluyt iii., 241].

March 25, 1543—Cartier present at a baptism in St. Malo [Quebec *Trans.*, 1862, p. 90].

Summer, 1543—Cartier brings Roberval back [Lescarbot and Que. *Trans.*, p. 93].

April 3, 1544—Cartier and Roberval summoned to appear before the King within eighteen days [Que. L. and H. S. *Trans.*, 1862, p. 94].